IN THEIR OWN WORDS

*Profiles of Today's
Chinese Students*

Tony Gallagher

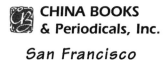

**CHINA BOOKS
& Periodicals, Inc.**

San Francisco

IN THEIR
OWN WORDS

First Edition 1998

Book and Cover Design by Linda Revel
Calligraphy by Inso Chung

Library of Congress Catalog Card Number: 98-71292

ISBN: 0-8351-2634-X

Printed in the United States of America by

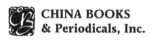 **CHINA BOOKS**
& Periodicals, Inc.

CONTENTS

AUTHOR'S NOTE   IX

PROLOGUE   XI

CHAPTER 1 Mr. Tony, Do Male Kangaroos Have
           Pouches?   1

CHAPTER 2 Home, Family, and Childhood   15

CHAPTER 3 Campus Life   39

CHAPTER 4 The Great Learning   59

CHAPTER 5 Youth and the Pursuit of Happiness   89

CHAPTER 6 The Love Thing   127

CHAPTER 7 China: Yesterday and Today   151

CHAPTER 8 China's Future, Our Future   185

POSTSCRIPT   213

AUTHOR'S NOTE

Wherever necessary, I have repaired the syntax and spelling in the students' essays you are about to enjoy. In doing so, I have left distinctive cultural and personal characteristics untarnished—such as in this apology note from a graduate student:

> *Dear Mr. Tony,*
>
> *I'd like you to give me a two-week off because my wife brings me a baby.*
>
> *Sincerely,*
>
> *Buck*

No actual names of Chinese students, teaching colleagues, or friends are used in this book.

Peking University, January 1993

JUST INSIDE PEKING UNIVERSITY'S WEST GATE is one of the campus' best-known pedestrian thoroughfares: a well-used, elegant stone bridge of ancient, imperial design that crosses over a rectangular reflection pond. For me, this bridge was to become the most meaningful sight on this beautiful campus. During my very first visit to Peking University in 1993 I paused at the bridge. Inexplicably, I knew at that moment that I would be unable to resist being drawn back there.

Yet the portents for this first encounter were initially inauspicious. Firstly, several months beforehand I had taken a rather unusual decision to have an eight-day winter holiday in Beijing on my own, while my family remained home in Canberra, Australia, leading normal lives. Secondly, on that day at the stone bridge, everything was frozen solid, the surrounding landscape looked somber, heavily draped with smog, and my Chinese host was in no mood to tarry. It was an extremely cold afternoon so she was more intent on briefly introducing me to some parts of the campus before returning to the warmth of her home as quickly as possible.

Despite her sense of urgency, I felt compelled to stop. Even today, four years later, I could show you the exact place and recapture my exact mood. Time stood still as, deep within me, a startling and seemingly ridiculous decision took hold: I like this place. I would love to work here. My children are grown up now. Why not quit my comfortable government job and teach English again?

The seeds for my encounter with China had been sown. Little did I know then, on the stone bridge just inside West Gate, just how vital my future students would become to my revised and better understanding of China, ancient and modern. Little did I know then just how strongly they would challenge my prejudices about them and their country and how I would learn from their insights. My students in fact, became my windows into China.

This book is my attempt to share what I have learned. It is a view into the private lives, into some of the innermost thoughts, feelings, hopes, and aspirations of a cross-section of undergraduate students at Peking University today—the post-Mao generation. Interspersed with my commentary and observations, this is their story.

CHAPTER 1

Mr. Tony, Do Male Kangaroos Have Pouches?

IN MID-SEPTEMBER, 1994, I faced an undergraduate English class at Peking University for the first time. Almost everything around me was strange and unfamiliar. I was nervous. What would I say to them?

I looked at the rows of silent, expectant faces. What were they thinking? All the rather useless Western propaganda about the Chinese people, which I had dutifully absorbed for over thirty years, went into instant replay. Could it be true? Did a communist ideology really possess the hearts and minds of all these students, setting role models for their conduct, prescribing their thoughts, and suppressing their individuality? What if I strayed from the content of their textbooks during class? Would I be denounced by them as a bourgeois rightist?

I had to relieve the tension somehow. After all, they were young adults—no more, no less—and I was just here to help them with their English. I needed to get them to relax, to begin to talk so that I could assess the level of their listening and speaking skills.

With the chalk in my left hand in my usual fashion, I wrote my name, "Dr. Tony Gallagher" on the blackboard. I heard gasps of surprise. In China, all students are taught to write with their right hands, regardless of their natural tendency, in order to write Chinese characters in the proper stroke order. I turned to face them again and said, "As my family name may be difficult for you to say, just call me Mr. Tony."

So, after these preliminaries, I asked them what they wanted to talk about. I was initially taken back by the directness of their response. They wanted to know about my family and why I had come to China. I explained that my two children were now grown up and independent. I said that after twenty-two years as a government official in the Australian Public Service I had decided, with the support of my wife, to fulfill a dream and come to China to teach for a while. I then invited them to practice their English by asking me anything about Australia.

Gradually the questions began. Soon there was a torrent and I found myself being asked anything and everything, including questions about kangaroos. They wanted to know how big they grew, how far they could jump, were they dangerous. A young woman student asked, "Where do baby kangaroos live?"

I replied, "From when they are very tiny, they live in their mother's pockets, or pouches."

Then, to my surprise, the next student asked, "Mr. Tony, do male kangaroos have pouches?"

For a moment my mind drew a complete blank as I realized that I was unsure of the answer. To maintain the pace of the rapport, I guessed and said, "No." As I gained confidence that my guess was correct, I began to see how their questions were achieving something quite tangible. I felt a connection to their world. What I did not realize was that later, mainly through further and deeper understanding of the thoughts and feelings of my students, most of my preconceptions about China were to fall away.

For nearly three years from that day I taught English and Australian Studies to undergraduate and graduate students. My students were bright and hard-working—competition to enter Peking University being extremely tough. As I was to discover, although most of them could not speak confidently, they all understood written English at a high level. The classes, averaging around 40 students, were drawn from various academic disciplines offered at the university, and comprised roughly equal numbers of young men and women.

It helped motivate me to think that I was lucky enough to be teaching some of China's future leaders: scientists, mathematicians, accountants, translators, computer consultants, businessmen and lawyers. Perhaps even future politicians and bureaucrats—perhaps not. Almost all of them claimed that they did not wish to work for the government on graduation. This saddened me as I knew every country needs political and bureau-cratic leaders of the very best quality.

I knew too that 1998 would be the landmark Centenary year of this distinguished university. Students of Peking University (known in China as *Beida*, an abbreviation of *Beijing Daxue*) inherit a special legacy. Throughout this century Beida has been a place of leadership during times of national protest. Some of these initiatives are remembered with pride, while some are not.

In the early 20th century, during the days of the last Qing dynasty emperor, Puyi, and the political fragmentation which followed his reign, some of China's emerging left-wing intellectuals came from Beida. One of those leaders was Li Dazhao, who worked as a librarian at Beida. He gave the young Mao Zedong a job in the library and influenced his political beliefs. At that time the main campus of Beida was in central Beijing, just east of the Forbidden City and an easy walk from a well-known contemporary landmark, Tiananmen Square. On May 4, 1919, over 3,000 patriotically-minded students from universities and colleges assembled at Tiananmen Gate, in front of the Forbidden City, to protest the unjust and disastrous Treaty of Versailles which, without Chinese consent, agreed to transfer German-held territories in Shandong Province to Japan.

After 1949, facilities near the Forbidden City were needed by the new Chinese government for administrative purposes. So, by 1953, Beida and other universities had been moved to the northwest outskirts of the city. Beida took over the buildings and grounds of an American missionary college known as Yancheng University. That is how Beida and the neighboring Tsinghua (Qinghua) University, the nation's leading engineering university, came to occupy part of the Qing dynasty gardens not far from the beautiful tourist attraction now known as the Summer Palace. In today's Beijing it is about a one hour struggle on a bicycle from Beida to the city center, or a little less if you take an impossibly crowded bus and then transfer to the subway.

With Beida's reputation for fostering the ideas of radical students, I wondered, could some of the students I was about to teach, these young people of the post-Mao generation, be political agitators? They were certainly post-Mao. They were all born within a few years of the death of Chairman Mao in 1976. They were post-Deng too, in a sense, as they would begin to graduate in 1997, after the death of Deng Xiao Ping. I hoped to avoid political agitators as, in attempting to understand the post-Mao generation, I did not wish to be deluded by words twisted with too much political passion. I was looking for different kinds of words. Words from the heart certainly, but words about what it meant to be young in modern China, especially words which expressed whether the ancient essences of China still meant anything.

Of the twenty or so universities I visited in China, Beida was the most beautiful. As well, it had an air about it of being a special place, of being first among peers, and with good reason. It had the largest number of Ph.D. programs and doctoral advisers. Among Chinese universities, Beida continues to be first in terms of awards for academic excellence. With its very high proportion of postgraduates, renowned professors and researchers, its considerable income derived from university owned companies and many foreign funded centers and scholarships, Beida deserves its place among the world's best universities. In fact, in May 1997, the magazine *Asia Review* listed Beida as the sixth best university in Asia. Of course, the variables used to measure "best" can always be contested. What was significant was that Beida was the only Chinese mainland university in the top ten, and was listed ahead of any Australian university.

But in so many ways it was not at all like the universities I had come to know so well during my career in the Australian Public Service. One clear difference was that the older rhythms of China seemed to pulsate so strongly in its daily life. For instance I discovered that for me and most of the university community mornings started early—classes commenced every day at 7:30 A.M. However, by about 11:30 A.M. most classrooms and offices were almost deserted and remained so until about 2:00 P.M. to allow us the opportunity of the traditional midday rest. Ah! I came to love that midday snooze!

Life went on round the clock as not only students but academics, other staff and their families lived on campus. As well, in the absence of nation-wide social welfare programs such as aged and health care in China, retired staff lived on campus too. One of the most delightful sights around my living quarters was to see toddlers being tenderly cared for by their often ex-professorial grandparents. In addition, because of the strong tradition of responsibility and respect in China towards the older generation, Beida, like other government enterprises, rarely fired workers or offered early retirement. In one sense the campus was more like a social welfare agency than a university; it operated rather like a small town, running profit-making enterprises and supporting schools, hospitals and subsidized entertainment. Low-cost housing, whereby nearly all staff members had apartments at peppercorn rentals, was abolished commencing 1996. From then, staff paid progressively higher rentals or were compelled to buy their apartments at reasonable prices.

In my English classes I discussed all kinds of things with the students. Topics such as: what makes for friendship; can love last; the dangers of riding bicycles; is tradition being crushed by technology; the merits of republicanism; the purposes of education; China's challenges and China's future; how to keep fit; and how to be more patient. I seized on anything, on any subject which would spark their interest to get them talking and hence practicing spoken English. I did this because I wanted them to believe that they had English skills sufficient to express their thoughts and feelings, not just echo others' thoughts. In return, they rewarded me one-hundredfold: through their talk and their writing they became my windows into China.

In late August 1994, when I was officially and warmly welcomed at Beijing Airport and escorted to Beida, I did not realize that I was about to be looked upon kindly by the Chinese gods. Usually overseas teachers, researchers, and students are assigned rooms at *Shaoyuan,* a huge and rather institutionalized residential complex on campus. I would have found the uniformity of such an environment suffocating. Instead, I was placed in the more exclusive North Guesthouse situated beside a pretty little lake in a secluded part of campus.

North Guesthouse had only 27 apartments—old but comfortable. During my time there usually about one-third of the foreign residents were Americans and the rest were from an assortment of other nations. We were all far from home. I came to be close friends with several, especially Rob and Shirley, an American couple, and Celia, a Chinese woman in her early thirties born in Hong Kong but raised in America. Celia was to teach me much about one Chinese way of looking at the world. I was to discover many others on my own. I was the only Australian at North Guesthouse; indeed, I was the sole Australian employed as a long-term Foreign Expert at Beida.

For a moment, I must advance a little in the chronology of my story to explain something. One evening during my third semester, two former students, Zhang and Ma, came to my apartment to talk (the students often did this, sometimes unannounced). One of the young visitors, Zhang, was from prosperous Zhejiang Province. However, she was not at all wealthy as her parents were very poor villagers. In class Zhang was rather shy and isolated from other students. As she was difficult to draw out, I made a special effort to reach her. Zhang's major was Physics and Ma, her friend, was majoring in Astronomy. Ma was the more self-assured of the two. This could have been partly the outcome of her family background as both her parents were engineers. Ma came from Guiyang, the capital of Guizhou, a poor province in the far south.

By the time this visit occurred I had been to cities in seven provinces in eastern and northern China. So, I thought I knew a little about China. Ma and Zhang were about to remind me otherwise. They began to talk about their families and the importance of Chinese cultural traditions in their lives. So I decided to mention that I had begun to write a book based on the feelings and opinions of my students at Beida. There was brief silence.

"You should not do this until you know us deeply," said Ma.

"How can you write this book unless you know Chinese?" said Zhang. "Until you can read Chinese you cannot understand our culture."

I told them I intended to go ahead as I wished to record my first impressions. I said it would be those impressions which would be the most meaningful to my friends and others I knew.

In my case the China I actually encountered was not at all like that which I had expected to see. It was a place of fascinations and frustrations, of paradoxes and delights. I knew for certain I would never fully understand it. But not only did I want to set down my initial impressions, I was motivated by something else as well. My encounter with China had strengthened my faith in the human spirit. And that was what gave me heart to write this book.

I came to a China facing the turmoil of modernization: rapid urbanization, massive changes in job patterns, the rise of individuality in the face of repression, the replacement of the extended family with the nuclear family, and the fracturing of traditional morality. I found that underneath the interminable political slogans such as "moving from a planned economy to a market economy" and "marching towards the world," China's economic transformation was indeed remarkable—both at national level and for individuals. For example, in 1995 I read an official claim in China's best-known English language newspaper, *China Daily,* that local currency savings of individuals in that year (as distinct from savings held in overseas currencies) were a whopping 26 times the 1979 figure. I noticed that a few individuals really did have money to burn. For the really well-off, travel agencies within China advertised weekend getaway holidays by air to resort cities like Chengdu in Sichuan Province or Xi'an in Shaanxi Province. Even the vast mass of ordinary people seemed to be doing better, and public works projects seemed to be getting increased funding. Booming port cities, such as Shanghai, ornamented with their glass-fronted buildings and neon lights, cities where foreign trade and industry got their start 100 years ago, were in the midst of a capitalist ferment.

It was a China where the nucleus of a middle class was emerging, as were semi-autonomous commercial power bases. Almost all of these continued to be dominated by direct or indirect government ownership, a parasitic relationship which gives the Western "market economy" special Chinese characteristics. So doing business here takes special patience, special skills.

Regardless, it was to my joy that I found my Chinese friends were able to carve out some personal space in their lives which was out of reach of the government. To my chagrin, I found that, as government salaries were so low, many university teachers, public officials and doctors were looking for extra ways of earning money. They were going into private business. (The Chinese call this *xiahai* or "jumping into the sea.") Yet, at the same time, they kept their regular jobs, their "iron rice bowl" with its job security, housing and health insurance. And sadly, from the media reports and countless personal stories, it seemed that everywhere in China too many officials at every level were on the take, dependent for additional incomes and benefits on the progress or perceived progress of reforms and on the improvement of the economy.

The China in which I lived and worked had many of the materialistic trappings of cities like Seattle, New York, Sydney, or Canberra. It had talk radio, joint ventures, personal checking accounts, a securities market, supermarkets, and private schools. Everywhere, and for everyone who could afford them, were McDonald's, Kentucky Fried Chicken, Pizza Hut, and Coca Cola. Even scratch-and-win lottery tickets were available.

With all these signs, I thought gloomily, wherever one went on earth at the end of the second millennium, the human race is ending up the same. Older social and cultural forces seemed have lost control: an insidious low-level international homogenization, driven by western-controlled consumerism and mass-media interests was swallowing up indigenous cultures making all of us insipid and identical. If so, there was no need for me to struggle earnestly within the confines of my own cultural milieu to understand a culture as different as China's. Its traditions and grassroots folklore were being rapidly swept away. Yet, under this gloss of advertising jingles, pop music, and modernization were signs that China was not the same at all. These signs were clear and strong.

For one thing, I knew my preferred approach to understanding a country as large and complicated as China was too simplistic. There was a lamentable lack of particularity in my mental image. More than a billion people lived'in China, yet they were involuntarily imprisoned within a sweeping generalization. I found it easier to consider all Chinese the same—even in the face of knowing that China stretches as far north to south as from Siberia to the Sahara and is peopled by almost one-quarter of humanity. Looking at Western civilization, I had no difficulty in making distinctions between peoples and parts. I recognized for instance that the one-quarter of humanity with whom I most readily identified lived in Europe and the Americas, in about 50 separate countries. But with China, I clung to my useless generalizations because it was too threatening to abandon it. Subconsciously underpinning it, perhaps, was a forlorn and arrogant hope that one day China might follow the Western political and social systems.

Secondly, for a long time China was (and to some extent, still is) a bureaucratic, agrarian empire. Even today, over 80 percent of the Chinese people lived in the countryside. Throughout a 5,000 year history, government, landlord and peasant have been tied into a self-perpetuating, hierarchical relationship. Because of the huge population (more than four times the population of the U.S., yet occupying only about half the cultivated area), farming has remained surprisingly primitive. Furthermore, although farming has foregone mechanization, for the most part it has remained remarkably efficient. Indeed, nowhere else on earth has such a proportion of humanity continued so successfully to feed itself and rise from poverty so rapidly.

I wondered if I could see the effects of these long-standing differences between Eastern and Western culture in my students. Or had socialist ideology and technology overrun traditional Chinese values? I wondered whether I could draw out my students' views and feelings, whether they would be willing to tell me how it felt to be Chinese. Although my students seemed warm-hearted it was hard to judge how open they were prepared to be. Because of their politeness it was difficult to predict how reticent they really would be when it came to sharing matters of the heart.

During my first attempts in class it seemed that, they preferred to maintain a culture of silence. Beyond the obvious facts that I was a teacher and a stranger to them, I knew there were good reasons for this. For the Chinese this has been a century of turmoil. The students have learned how important it is not to get themselves (and their family members) into trouble. It was as if, in the back of their minds, they were always aware of the Chinese proverbs that say, "The gun always hits the bird flying first" and "The roof beam that sticks out is the first to rot."

Yet, was their politeness solely a defense mechanism, a survival skill resulting from generations of repression? They seemed to possess something more, something with deeper, older roots, something subtle and rather difficult to define. It was a politeness and a genius for understatement, beautifully illustrated in a well-known Chinese legend from the Song dynasty (960-1,279 A.D.):

> There was a talented scholar by the name of Sun Shan who was known for his rich sense of humor. One year Sun Shan was preparing set off to sit for an imperial examination when a villager asked him if he wouldn't mind accompanying his son who was leaving for the same purpose. So, the two young men journeyed together.
>
> When the list of successful candidates was published the villager's son turned out to be a failure. Sun Shan's name was, by good fortune, the last one on the list. Sun Shan hurried home with the good news. On the way he met the villager who was extremely anxious and asked him about his son's fortune. Sun Shan replied indirectly, in verse:
>
> > *Sun Shan is at the end of the name list*
> > *Your worthy son comes after Sun Shan.*

Standing before what seemed like a wall of courtesy, how could I hope to be successful in my search for the inner signs of my students' cultural legacy? I decided to try in the way I knew best. I would encourage them to share their thoughts and feelings in writing. I assured them that they would be writing for me alone. I promised I would not reveal the content of their essays by referring to them in classes. It worked. Later it occurred to me to write this book. So I told the students about my decision and asked those with the most interesting essays to rewrite their work. Many agreed to do this.

After each lesson, when I corrected my students' writings I realized that, because they were at the threshold of adulthood, most of them had not yet learned to disguise their real feelings. They had not learned to contrive clever but hollow words which would merely flatter a reader's tastes or expectations. Instead, their writings were honest and direct. It was truly refreshing to come upon so many novel ideas or unexpected but delightful turns of phrase. They seemed to have a knack of combining English words in different ways than would native speakers. Through these windows into the private lives of the post-Mao generation I was becoming young again. To my joy I began to see how deeply they loved their culture.

CHAPTER 2

Home, Family, and Childhood

I love these people and I feel so happy to own their love. It is said that it is intellect that distinguishes mankind from lower animals. I want to say that it's our intelligent love that adds to our lives more substance than that of the lives of the lower animals.

—Zhao Ying ♦ *Geology* **♦ HEILONGJIANG PROVINCE**

MANY OF OUR DEEPEST FEELINGS are about home and family. This was also true for my Beida students. Yearning for home and fond childhood memories were strong themes in their writings. Often they acknowledged a debt of gratitude to their parents: they knew only too well the great sufferings endured by previous generations.

I knew of these sufferings too. Back home in Australia in the early 1990s, through movies such as *The Joy Luck Club* and biographical stories such as *Wild Swans*, millions of us had become familiar with stories of endurance and hardship in China. Such stories are known in China as the "Literature of the Wounded." Once I began teaching there, such stories of suffering were all around me. This intensified, rather than diminished, the impact.

Take for example Wu Chun's family story. Wu, a young teacher in the English Department, was at one time assigned to look after my routine administrative needs. We came to know one another well. One day she grumbled to me about the low level of teachers' salaries and the general inconsiderateness of governments. Then to my surprise she went deeper. She said she hated the government. She could never forget that when she was a small child she had witnessed the execution of her grandfather. He had been mayor of a town in central China and had been shot simply because he was on the Kuomintang side when the Communists took over. Then there was another teacher, Wang Su. Before 1949 her grandfather had been a small landowner in Shandong Province. He moved to Shanghai rather than suffer public humiliation and be criticized merely for being a landlord but, she told me, events caught up with him and he was arrested. He died in prison, probably of starvation.

In the early 1950s, when the grandparents of the post-Mao generation were young adults, the world found China's drive to become a great nation rather awesome. By 1953 inflation had been halted, industry nationalized, and production restored to previous levels. Land had been taken from landlords and redistributed among the peasants via farming collectives. Then came the unhinging of common sense. Chairman Mao tolerated no opposition to his leadership nor to his flawed blueprint to liberate the peasantry from poverty, disease, and malnutrition. In June 1957, commencing with the Great Leap Forward and ending with the anti-rightist campaign, China entered a period of chaos known as the Great Leap Forward. It culminated in the grim three-year famine from 1959 which affected almost all of China's population.

In their turn, the parents of the post-Mao generation became young adults at a time of one of history's most bizarre events—the Great Proletarian Cultural

Revolution. The decade from 1966 to 1976 became lost years for China, lost years for many of my students' parents.

In the 1930s, thirty years before the Cultural Revolution, the brilliant Chinese writer Lu Xun had written bitter stories about the sadistic tendency to mock the misery of others. (The same Lu Xun, incidentally, won a logo design competition for Peking University in the 1920s, and this beautiful design is still used today.) Chairman Mao's Cultural Revolution organized social sickness on a massive public scale. The education system became crippled and was shut down. An open season began on anyone suspected of "taking the capitalist road" (pro-Western), or "being revisionist" (pro-Soviet). These unfortunates included many Chinese who had returned after 1949 to help China—such as Wu and Li who wrote about their personal tragedies in their well-known book *A Single Tear.* Young students and workers broke into the homes of the affluent, intellectuals, and officials, pointlessly destroying books and manuscripts, beating and killing occupants. Millions of innocent people were detained for "struggle meetings" where they were denounced and publicly humiliated.

The consequences were terrible and widespread; everywhere people were prepared to pay almost any price to survive. I recall all this history so that you may understand at a deeper level what I came to understand from my students. As one of my female students once said to me:

> Dad's fine on the outside, but the Party has destroyed him on the inside.

> He has no courage.

Perhaps, and this may possibly have been beyond her youthful experience, like so many others her father had learned that, in extreme circumstances, endurance itself can be noble. Indeed, endurance can be a kind of courage, sometimes superior to the raw courage required in battle.

One result of the disastrous Cultural Revolution was disillusionment with the socialist government and a renewal of reliance on the family. As Celia, my Chinese friend at Peking University's North Guesthouse once acutely observed, "Older Chinese have had enough of suffering." Now, they seemed to care little for governments and ideology; they just want to make a little money and do what is best for their children.

This sentiment can be seen in the students' stories on family, life, and childhood, which now follow:

MY FAMILY

I saw a photograph of my family when I looked through the photo album the other day. Before I left home and came to study here, little did I realize that my parents were the dearest teachers and friends of mine. Looking back, I come to understand that it is my family that makes me what I am now.

Unlike a traditional Chinese family, mine is a rather modest one, only my parents and myself. It also differs from a traditional one in that paternalism was never there. Even when I was little my parents encouraged me to follow what proved to be right, not just what they said. Opportunities were given to me to make my own decisions, provided that I could advance plenty of reasons. I remember once how they managed to give me consent when I asked to spend my vacation alone at home instead of traveling with them. At that time I was eleven. They tried to persuade me at first, but finally when I mentioned that it was a chance to plant ideas of independence in my mind and after all, it was my first important decision; they said 'yes' and gave me some useful tips before leaving.

In this kind of atmosphere, it became a rule that an important decision wouldn't be made unless we all approved it. I really enjoyed speaking out my mind and sharing an outlook on such matters with them, for it filled me with confidence and convinced me of my own ability.

This is only part of what my family gave me. The splendid world of knowledge would not lie before me now if my parents had not awakened the window on it. I would have lost heart if they had not offered their hands to me. I stagger in this unknown world and struggle to make progress, but with the conviction that my family are always backing me up. It is a never-empty spring of support and strength, an invaluable treasure in my heart.

However, it does not follow that independence is ignored. In fact it is the reverse. Most of the time, my family is only a lighthouse of hope in the distance, which protects me against the wrong course in the navigation of my life. I have to push myself hard to attain my goals.

Instead of giving me details of the solution to a problem they only point out the direction and leave the task of solving it up to me. They emphasized the courage to face difficulties, largely because of their rough experiences when they were younger. Their potential couldn't be realized as the result of the strangling of society in the past few decades, yet they gave me a message to keep alert to the brutal facts and face life with courage, which I can stake my whole life on.

—**Feng Huibin**
Geology
HUBEI PROVINCE

MY "CHILDREN"

Unfortunately I was the one and only child of my parents and was destined to lead a lonely life from childhood to adulthood without any sisters or brothers. That's the reason why I love little animals so much.

I used to have a tortoise, chickens, a goldfish, birds and rabbits. I tried my best to give them my love, a human's love, which may have been unsuitable for them. I fell into deep sorrow at their deaths, a human's real sadness. Since my parents couldn't put up with my tears, they forbade me from buying anything alive.

"That you may one day have a tiger with you in your home is none of our business; however, you can't have a living thing in our home." That was their saying. Living under the control of such bossy parents is my bad luck—although they are always democratic except on this matter. But there is nothing I can do under such circumstances.

The price of pets in Beijing has increased sharply. A tortoise which cost 1 yuan four years ago is 20 yuan today. Since I cannot afford to buy one, my boyfriend bought a couple of them for me. I knew clearly that my parents would surely be angry at my two "kids," because they were not only ugly but also expensive. The seller told me one was a male the other a female. I called them Wu Wu and Wen Wen respectively, which means powerful and intelligent. I like my "son" more than my daughter, treating Wu Wu much more affectionately than Wen Wen.

Wen Wen had such a good appetite that she could eat fish twice as quickly as Wu Wu could. She opened her big mouth biting the fish, tearing it and swallowing into her stomach. At first I could bear her greedy behavior. But before long, I began to scold her, "Shut up! Don't you feel ashamed?" To my disappointment, Wu Wu ate only a little or sometimes nothing at all. Then an idea jumped into my mind: separation!

Every time I fed them, all the fresh fish were provided for Wu Wu. Whenever he finished his meal it was Wen Wen's turn to eat the remaining food. Such a policy was a bit brutal, for Wen Wen could smell the fish but couldn't eat it. Feeling worried, anxious, she crawled here and there, searching every corner, but in vain. Her small eyes, which were like green beans, stared at me full of sadness, as if she said:

"Mum, why are you so unfair to me?"

My heart sank for I came to know I had no valid reason to punish her.

Now they are hibernating in the sand. Whenever I come back home, I will dip my finger into sand to touch their shells. They are sleeping sweetly and deeply. I'm eagerly awaiting their coming out in the spring.

My dream is that one day I will feed a couple of chickens, a little duck, one brown dog and two tortoises—my future family. I will be the manager of the "zoo" while my husband is the assistant.

—**Zhang Yang**
Law
BEIJING

A Country Childhood

To me, childhood is like a lotus, which grows up and blooms over the water by taking nourishment from the slush in the river. Because of its purity, refreshing fragrance, and elegance, childhood will be always blooming in my memory.

I was born and grew up in the country. I value my life in the country highly, for all my childhood was spent there. We had an old house around which were many pear trees. I liked their white flowers from a very young age and there was no doubt that I liked pears very much. In summer I always climbed up the tree, sat on the boughs and ate as many pears as I liked. Then I would lie lazily on the boughs, watching the beautiful clouds through the chinks of the green leaves and think my own stories. I enjoyed it so much that I could spend most of the day in the tree. When on the ground. I would tell the chickens stories, or teach my little cat dancing, though she didn't like it at all. There was no word "lonely" in my world even though I am the only daughter of my parents. I owe this to closeness to nature.

But living in the country didn't mean I could play and enjoy myself all the time. When I was about seven I began to know that we were poor. We had a debt of more than 1,000 yuan from dividing up the family property. My parents' total monthly income was about 50 yuan. So, at that time the debt was really a big sum.

Father lost the chance of going to college because of China's Cultural Revolution and had to work as a carpenter. Mother had to do almost all the housework because father could only come back on weekends. So I told myself I should help them as much as I could. Mother worked in a factory. In addition, she cultivated land and raised pigs, chickens, and sheep when she came back from work, so that we could pay all our debts.

I was sorry to see that mother had to cook the meals even though she was very tired after a day's heavy work. Then when I was eight, I gave mother the first big surprise. I cooked the dinner one evening. She said nothing but smiled at me and ate as if she had never had so good a meal, though I had turned the rice into porridge because I had put in too much water. I was proud of preparing dinner and from then on I did become one member of my family, for we three faced all the difficulties together. We were poor but we were happy for we all loved each other. When I was eleven we had paid all the debts and built one of the most beautiful houses in our village. Today, I cherish the hard times we had together for I have learned to be brave and calm while facing difficulties, and how to love persons who love me.

Living in the country also means you can become narrow-minded, self-satisfied, and opinionated. Father avoided this by constantly striving to improve himself. Though he was a carpenter, he loved reading and he saved every cent he could to buy good books. I remember once he spent 29 yuan to buy a dictionary, which was his whole wage for one month.

The thing he hated most was spoiling or losing books. But when I became a school student, I began to lend all the picture books he bought for me. Gradually I lost a big part of them. On knowing that, father flew into such a big fury that he claimed he would burn all the other picture books. He then set fire to them before me. I cried over the flames and thought desperately that he would never buy me a book again. During the next several days I always thought of those books. How I wished I could have them back again! And I did get them back. The next week-end when father returned home, he took out the books magically and told me that he only burnt some pieces of waste paper. He didn't say anything more about it.

Even today I still warn myself not to spoil books and never to lose them, for books widen one's vision, enrich one's mind, and give one more opportunities. Father knew it clearly when he was only a carpenter—he never stopped reading and studying. So when opportunities knocked at the door, he was ready. When I was in Grade I, father became a college student in the News Department of the People's University of China. His dream was to be a writer and now he has mostly realized it: he is a reporter.

Father never told me that you should study hard, but from a very young age I had known that I must struggle for what I want and never give up things easily. Father had taught me that. I carried this faith from the village middle school to one of the best senior schools of Hunan Province, and now carry it here, to be a student in the International Economics Department.

—Shao Yue
International Finance
HUNAN PROVINCE

MY CHILDHOOD

A lot of people say that childhood is the happiest time in one's life. I don't know whether it is true; however, I really treasure the memories of my childhood. I can remember many scenes clearly.

I spent nearly five years in kindergarten. I went there at the age of two, which was the required age. I had to go, for my parents were both in regular work and they had no time to look after me. It was the first time I left home. I kept on crying so hard on our way there that my mother even couldn't hold me in her arms. When we arrived, I struggled to run away, and fell prone on the slope. I refused to stand up. My mother forced me up and pushed me into the kindergarten. But when she went out, I followed her. She forced me in again. This sad little action was repeated three or four times. I couldn't understand why my mother was so cruel. Now, I know that she was looking on in agony at my sufferings at that moment, but she couldn't help me, for she had no choice. I consider it a real beginning of my life, because I began to know life is hard; sometimes we can fight against it, but sometimes we have to endure.

There were some jujube (date) trees in the garden of my kindergarten. One afternoon, the teacher told us the fruits had already matured and all of us would go out to pick them. We were very happy. We shook and kicked the trees, and picked up the jujubes which fell down. I concentrated on the work too much to pay attention to what was happening around me. I kept kicking the trees for a long time. Then I heard someone call me. I turned back, and found my teacher standing behind me. It was already dark and there was no one else in the garden except we two.

She said with a smile on her face, "All the other children have already entered the room, washed and eaten the jujubes. I found you were not in, so I hurried out to look for you."

I gave her a shy smile. Later, she praised me, not because I was so eager for the jujubes, but because my attitude towards work was serious.

She told us that one must concentrate on the work one is doing.

To some degree, I wasn't as happy as the children of today. I had less delicious food and less beautiful clothes. Although I like dolls very-much, I hadn't one, for my family used to be poor. But I didn't consider it a bitter life, for I was enriched by great love from my parents. They were frugal and tried their best to meet my needs. When the festivals came, my mother always made new clothes for me by hand. In summer, when it was very hot, my father used to fan me until I was fast asleep. I greatly appreciated them as it was they who brought happiness to my childhood. Being poor is not terrible, but life without love is. In fact, the poor life benefited me. It made me know how hard life can be.

—**Yang Zhanglan**
Sociology
SHANDONG PROVINCE

DURING MY LIFE IN CHINA I found it was not at all difficult to get access to people's family lives. I met many Chinese families and with them I shared happy times and ate lots of delicious meals. For the most part, these were ordinary urban Chinese families, or *laobaixing* (old one hundred surnames), as the Chinese would say. But it seemed impossible to stay in a family home as an overnight or weekend guest. This was partly because Chinese apartments are small but, insofar as I could tell, it also manifested a government prohibition.

One Chinese family I knew very well lived in North China—in burgeoning Dalian, the port city of Liaoning Province. For nearly 20 years while working in Canberra, I had exchanged letters with the Zheng family, particularly via their son, Xin Bao. Through these letters I learned that many aspects of suburban family life in

China were similar to my own family life; much of what I learned by letter was not reflected in media propaganda, whether Chinese or Australian. At the commencement of my second year of teaching, to my great satisfaction, I was able to visit the Zheng family.

As I wanted to practice my Chinese, I asked to stay in their home or the home of friends, but was unable to do so. Zheng was a Communist Party member and maybe this was the reason. But, even if they had wished to invite me, there was no room as Xin Bao, his wife Xiao Jing, and their five-year old daughter also squeezed into the apartment.

As is the case with families everywhere, the Zheng family did not always live in sweet harmony. Over lunch one day Xin Bao admitted that living in close quarters with his parents was very stressful; too often quarrels over trifling matters occurred between his mother and his wife. He also found, even though he was over 30, it was still hard to bridge the generation gap between himself and his father, especially over matters of careers and money. Despite these difficulties, his loyalty to the concept of the family unit was unshakable as was his sense of social obligation to all family members.

The strength of such family ties is reflected in the following three stories.

MY FATHER

In my childhood, I often got punished by my father for reasons which have slipped my mind long ago. At that time, I hated him a lot, and I even thought of someday when I would be able to change my father. But now, in my twenties, when I am a sophomore of Peking University, I owe thanks to my father, my dear father. Given the hardness of those days, I can understand him now.

I am the youngest of the six children in my family. Such a big family made a heavy burden on him. In spite of all hardships he did not try to wash his hands of us. When I was twelve he enrolled my three brothers and me into the same middle school. That is still an incredible thing even today when people's living conditions are greatly improved. He could have had some of my brothers drop out of school so that the burden was light enough for him to shoulder. But he did not do so, perhaps, never thought so. He knew well that to have a better life we must get education.

Every year, when the new semester began, he managed to collect enough money to meet our tuition. Maybe he borrowed it from someone. I never knew and he never said. His income was so poor that essential living needs were a problem. At that time my mother and my two sisters were unemployed, and father was the only support of my family. I can't imagine how he pulled my family through those years. Now, when my family's living conditions have been greatly improved he never reminds us of how hard he worked those days. He seems to take it for granted.

Why did he beat me in those days? Maybe the hard life gave him a bad temper. Maybe I was a naughty boy. I don't intend to look into it now. After all, that did not prevent him from being a good father.

—**Nie Xiaoping**
Physics
SHAANXI PROVINCE

DEAR BROTHER

I have not heard from you for several months. How are things?

On my book case lies the cassette which belongs to you. It always reminds me of the day when you brought me to this university. Remember? You selected a series of books from your box for me. You put the cassette into my bag and asked me to train my English listening skills. You offered me the recorder, which still lies on my shelf. You bought it when you were in Nanjing University, with the fellowship you earned. You told me that you were very sorry to have to give me a used recorder, for you couldn't afford a new one.

Do you still remember our past? In those days I was "the tail" of you. I followed you everywhere, because I hadn't anyone to play with. But you were 6 years older than me and certainly you didn't want to be my partner. So you always went all out to get rid of me. However, I just kept track of you, and found you every time. Usually this continued until you were out of temper and beat me, and I began to cry. I cried not because of pain but rather intending to draw Mama's attention—she would revenge me. Usually this ended with you covering my mouth and comforting me with the tenderest words you could speak and the most shining smile you could smile. Then, you became helpless, confronted with the fact that I followed you everywhere, though you extremely disliked this!

Recalling the past always makes me smile. Christmas Day is coming now. I wish to hear from you in a few days, and say to you "MERRY CHRISTMAS."

Yours,

Brother

December 10, 1995

—Jia Jiantao
History
JIANGSU PROVINCE

MY GRANDMOTHER

My grandmother took care of me for several years when I was a little boy. I can't forget her even though she has been dead for so many years.

She was an amicable old woman. She seldom lost her temper and she loved me deeply. I still remember that every time I irritated her, instead of beating me, she would tap her forehead angrily. She was also very kind to others and was ready to help them.

My grandmother was an industrious woman. She got up very early every day. She prepared meals for the family and also did a lot of hard work. Father told me that after my grandmother married she had worked hard to support the family. And because of the work, she was very healthy. She died of cancer at the age of eighty.

My grandmother couldn't bear loneliness. When she was alone at home, she often invited some old women from the village to our house and then played mahjong. She always had a good time with them. It seems that people in China can't live in solitude in the same way as in other countries.

Now she has left me forever, but her influence on me doesn't end. I still have a good memory of her and miss the times when I was with her. I miss her good character.

—Li Haitao
Geophysics
ANHUI PROVINCE

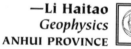

THE GRANDMOTHER in the last story by Li Haitao possessed three desirable characteristics: she was amicable, industrious and gregarious. Sometimes, perhaps rather unfairly, I would ask my students or Chinese friends to tell me what they thought were the three best Chinese characteristics, and the three worst. Usually, after a painful struggle, the best three they chose were contained in words similar to prudence, loyalty, responsibility, diligence, capability, and kindness. And the worst? They were chosen from words like vanity, indifference, aimlessness, laziness, graft, secrecy, and cruelty.

I have my own Chinese story about grandparents, home, and family. In the middle of my first semester, through rather unusual circumstances, I became close friends with Chen Fusheng, the honorary grandfather of one of my students, Yan Fan. (Chen had been "adopted" by Yan Fan's family when she was a little kid, as at that time she had no living natural grandfathers.)

Chen, who lived far from Beijing in a home for destitute old folks, had written a letter asking me to help "Dawn Swallow," as he called Yan, with her English. As it proved, she needed little help. But so began a series of over 50 amazing letters in which Chen told me much about family, childhood, and the sufferings of his generation. At the end of second semester I decided to journey to Zhejiang Province to meet this interesting man and we had long chats about his remarkable life. Through Chen's letters during the rest of my time in China, I was strengthened again and again by his dignity and determination not to yield under the most difficult personal circumstances.

Chen had learned his English mainly through self-instruction. As fate would have it, he had translated for the Kuomintang beginning in the late 1930s and then during the 1940s. So, after 1949, he suffered denouncements and public humiliations when he returned to his village.

Chen told me of the black days during the Cultural Revolution when foolish and futile efforts to improve crop yields by young party cadres in his village led to famine, and of how he and others were forced to ransack graves for timber, stone, and iron. In one letter he described the humiliation he, as a "bad element," had to suffer in late 1969, after the unfairly disgraced and deposed President of China, Liu Shaoqi, died in prison:

THE HEAD OF ALL "BAD EGGS"

After his death, I, the head of all bad eggs, was compelled by the village security guard to put on a strange-looking hat made of bamboo strips pasted all round with yellowish paper on which had been written anti-Liu slogans.

A single column parade composed of bad elements with me walking slowly in front was to pass houses in different neighboring villages. We were to be a funeral procession to curse the dead criminal Liu Shaoqi. The village security guard went before me holding above his head a wooden cut-out figure of a Western-style small dog with a gigantic red nose symbolizing Liu Shaoqi.

During the parade he ordered me to strike a brass gong. As I had no experience, I struck once, and about a minute later I made the second strike.

"Oh no! Not like that! The funeral gong should not be struck so slowly. Can't you do anything right! Strike it quicker."

So I hit it every few seconds.

"No, no. It's too fast! Hit it every five paces."

I did as I was bid.

"Now it's OK," agreed the guard. "Now keep on striking."

I struck for a whole day except for a temporary pause for lunch.

Villagers came out of their houses to see what was happening. Some looked with suspicious eyes, some were quiet. Some stretched their necks, to look from behind others' backs, many giggling ceaselessly. They did not understand what we were doing and neither did I. The whole situation seemed to clarify one thing: Liu Shaoqi was a very bad fellow, so bad that not only good people disliked him, but we bad elements as well.

—Chen Fusheng
Meishan Old Folks' Home
XIAOSHAN, ZHEJIANG PROVINCE

WHERE WAS "HOME" to my students? Because Beida's competitive selection system incorporated quotas of a few of the very best students from all Provinces and regions, usually they came from every part of China—except one. Shanghai students generally preferred to remain in their home city as, rightly or wrongly, they considered the Shanghai education system and lifestyle to be superior to that of any other city. I did teach a few students from Shanghai on scholarships at Beida, but they were largely outnumbered by the others. Thus, my classrooms were a microcosm of China, containing as they did people from all over the country, young people possessing very different backgrounds and traditions. Some were sophisticated city kids from large inner or coastal cities. Others were from villages or towns somewhere in the upper or lower Yangtze River delta—the world's largest food producing region for over 200 years, a vast area of green crop land and patches of great beauty, dotted with hundreds of lakes and crisscrossed by canals. Others were from more mountainous country further up the Yangtze River valley beyond Wuhan in Hubei Province, or near Chongqing in Sichuan. The homeland of others was the mountains or high table-lands to the far south in Guizhou or tropical parts of neighboring Yunnan. Others hailed from the dry, cold steppes of Qinghai or the deserts of Xinjiang to the North West. Others had their homeland somewhere in the yellow North China plain or the harsh, tough mountains of Shanxi Province to Beijing's immediate west.

Because of these huge differences the kind of "home" described in the next story cannot be seen as typical. Tang Ming's little home town in Southern Fujian has an idyllic, dreamlike quality. Not all villages are like this, but the sentiment, the fondness for home, was almost universal.

MY HOMETOWN

When Chinese people say "my hometown," they refer to where they are born or where they spent their childhood. My hometown is a little town in Fujian Province in the southeast of China. It's so tiny that you can't find it on the most detailed map. But it's so beautiful that I won't forget it in all my life.

Have you seen films about little towns south of the Yangtze River in China? Just like these towns, my hometown is located on two banks of one small river. A street crosses the town and there are many alleys among the houses. All the houses in this town are small and made of wood. A little bridge made of stones crosses the river. This is what my hometown is like when you first see it—ordinary and quiet.

But I have to say it is just this quietness that make this little town unique. All the roads are made of big stones. The stones are as old as three or four hundred years. They are so old that they have become very slippery. And it would be interesting for you to walk in the alleys winding among the little old wooden houses during the rain. You would hear the sound of rain falling on the stones and the sound of your shoes stepping on them.

The tunes are just like music played by nature. Perhaps you don't bring an umbrella with you. Don't worry. You will find one door open nearby the streets. Suddenly a face filled with smiles invites you in for hot tea.

The little river is also graceful. The water is green. There are always two or three old men standing on the little bridge fishing. They are so absorbed that no one passing by disturbs them. They usually set the fish free since they only enjoy the sport of fishing.

Evening in my hometown is also beautiful. Under the yellow half-moon, large and low, you will see the light glisten in every house and white smoke arise slowly into the darkness. At that time, you will touch the excitement of the people of town who have just worked hard for the day. You will hear talking and laughter. Can you imagine?

My town! It is so good. I hope to go back to it one day.

—**Tang Ming**
Chemistry
FUJIAN PROVINCE

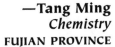

MANY OF MY STUDENTS were far from home and had not previously been separated from their family and loved ones for such an extended period. From time to time some of them became wistful and homesick. This yearning for home is reflected in this last story. Chen Pei tells us about her homeland, beautiful Guilin in the far south of China.

 MY DEAREST HOMELAND

I am sitting on my bed, looking at the full moon in the star-dotted black sky of Beijing. Are my parents and sister looking at the same moon in Guilin? Oh, how I love them. The moonlight is shining like flowing water throughout the serene campus. Are all the beautiful hills and rivers in my homeland being covered in the moonlight like here, now? Oh, how I love them too! That is my land, bearing my dearest folks and dearest hills and rivers.

I was lucky enough to be born in Guilin, the world-famous beauty-spot. Its extraordinary scenery is inherently part of me ever since my childhood. The Li Jiang River is so serene, so green, so clear, so fresh, with the Elephant's Trunk Hill standing up in it, vividly like an elephant putting its nose in the wonderful water, thirstily drinking. It has become a symbol of the city of Guilin.

What's most precious to me is the Guilin folks that've brought me up, instructed me and have accompanied me through my childhood and my dearest teachers, my lovely younger sister and my little friends. When I dream of them and then wake up, I miss them so much. How could I forget them? How could I leave them?

But just for them, I've left my dearest homeland and am here to finish my own study. My homeland needs to be developed. Her young sons and daughters are out in their places of study, but they all bear in mind their dearest homeland.

—**Chen Pei**
Biology
GUANGXI AUTONOMOUS REGION

CHEN PEI'S STORY, especially her being reminded of home by the moon, is reminiscent of the famous poem *Lonely Thoughts on a Frosty Night*, by the Tang poet Li Bai, who lived in the eighth century:

Before my bed a pool of light
Can it be frost upon the ground?
Eyes raised, I see the moon so bright
Head bent, in homesickness I'm drowned

From time to time during my first year in China I became somewhat homesick and lonely. This was not surprising for during my marriage of 30 years I had not been apart from my wife, Annette, and two adult children, Lucy and Christian, for such a long period. When I told some students and Chinese friends about this they understood immediately and quoted a Chinese idiom about merchants and officials long ago who left their loved ones behind in order to work in the far south of China. The proverb said: "I face to the north." In my case, they said they would change the idiom for me: "Mr. Tony faces to the south."

CHAPTER 3

Campus Life

To some degree the dorm can even take part of the role of the family, though the members are the same age, same sex, same social background. Fortunately I am such a lucky one. Each time when I get depressed or come back from the classroom exhausted, I am always met by an atmosphere of ease, always a joke or a smile and that's enough.

There are also dorms full of jealousy, malice, grudges, and all sorts of things. This kind of air seriously interferes with their study and their making friends. One of my friends is in such a position and she is now very dreary.

The most essential function of the dorm is to provide a necessary course to socialize and mature. Keeping harmony with others is a complicated skill. Sometimes we have to reconcile with others. Inevitably, there will be things we encounter which we do not expect and we are reluctant to accept them. In such circumstances, in order to create a healthy, comfortable, easy-going environment, we have to make some effort to alter properly and modestly.

—Dong Lan ♦ *Philosophy* ♦ HUNAN PROVINCE

ONE OF MY supportive links to Australia was through friends at the Australian Embassy, with several of whom I had worked in Canberra. Every now and then, when I needed a break from the China experience, or I wanted an opportunity to catch up with Australian media news or useful gossip from home, I would visit the Embassy.

A month or so after my arrival in China I had a reunion with one of these Australian friends, the political Counselor, Jack Reid. I trusted Jack and wanted his advice. Jack's wife, Xia Wei, is Chinese and he has spent most of his public service career either in China or working on Chinese affairs while in Australia. My initial encounters with China had been rather overwhelming so I asked Jack to give me three simple maxims for survival. He said:

"First, keep healthy—you're only as good as your stomach. Second, expect the unexpected. Third, take one day at a time."

He was right, especially when it came to affairs of the stomach. Although almost every kind of food was available it was of variable and rather unpredictable quality. Eventually I came to really enjoy ordinary Chinese food, but for the first few months I found the change in diet difficult. Although I didn't know it at the time, my stomach was reacting to toxicity brought on by overdoses of artificial flavor enhancers, color additives, and monosodium glutamate.

For a while food became a preoccupation.

During the second semester I tutored two young "model workers" in English for about one month. As a reward for their diligence and patriotism, these two were attending the Chinese Institute of the Workers Movement, a kind of trade union college, located not far from Beida. Xie and Zhang knew little English, which, in turn, helped my Chinese. They were also very boisterous and much more direct than my Beida students. They simply laughed gleefully at my outrageous Chinese pronunciation and grammar. Xie and Zhang liked to bring me food as a present. It was through them that I was introduced to an awful mauve-colored imitation ice-cream and sticky Chinese dough sticks covered in cheap animal fat, peanuts and sesame seeds. Once they took me to a Chinese fast-food outlet near campus called "The Boss" where the salad was unrecognizable and hamburgers were so unbelievably horrible I was unable to eat them. Ugh!

After our lesson one day they asked me what food I would like next time we met, so I dauntlessly asked for cake or biscuits imagining at the time the delicious cakes my wife Annette made on weekends, back home in Canberra. When Xie and Zhang arrived the following week they had forgotten about the cakes. Instead with much pride, they presented me with some cold sticks of fatty Shandong pork and packaged dog meat. I remembered what Jack said: expect the unexpected; live one day at time. So I thanked them and we began the English lesson. I gave the dreadful packages to other student visitors at the next available opportunity.

Before I came to China I had difficulty in imagining what day-to-day life in a one party nation would be like. At first sight, as a visitor (or in my case as a privileged foreign guest worker), marriage and family, work and play resemble that of a more open society. The difference comes in interpersonal relations where a hierarchy of authorities gives some people power over others, although control is not as oppressive as it has been. In China a work unit, or *danwei*, keeps a confidential set of documents on everyone's achievements and conduct. In the students' case the work unit is the university and it controls allocation to academic disciplines, accommodation, educational opportunities, entertainment and, on paper at least, approval to marry, have sex, or bear children. The students are well aware of this.

Part of this attitude is Communist-inspired but it also contains older traditions. For the past twenty-five centuries Confucian thought has emphasized the need for the individual to be subordinate to the group, for the individual to fit into the larger scheme of things. In a sense, Confucian tradition can be seen as a kind of religion of law and order. Just as in the universe the sun, moon, and stars move according to the laws of nature, so a person too, should live within the framework of world order. In contemporary, overpopulated China such figuring still makes much sense. For the students, living on campus becomes a practical lesson in the Chinese way of doing things, an initiation into the Chinese adult world. The lessons learned from campus life are at least as important as formal classes. Of course, for some, like Liu Jian, this adjustment can be a pleasant opportunity to be creative.

DECORATING MY LIVING SPACE

Not until I moved my bed upward to the bed over my previous one, did I find I was interested in the design and decorating of my own living space.

There are five girls living in our small dormitory, and we have three two-storeyed beds. I have lived in the bottom storey. And I've thought it was convenient, because I could reach everything on my bed easily and sit on the edge without taking off my shoes. If living above, one needs to climb up and down and take off shoes all along in order not to make the bed beneath dirty. Sleeping in a high place was also frightening to me.

But I've been through many awful things in the first year in the Biology Department.

Everything on my bed or beside my bed or on the wall was so familiar to me and made me feel I was still in that awful year. So I felt depressed. Also I didn't like my previous way of decorating my bed. So, one Saturday afternoon, I suddenly made up my mind to move upward. As I am a determined girl, doing things without too many useless thoughts, I began taking action immediately. I decided to arrange everything to my own flavor, so that I could feel the new beginning of my life.

Maybe there are too many things, but I arranged them well and neatly. The quilt was put at one end of the bed. Beside it and close to the wall, I put a blue plastic shelf with several Chinese novels. My tapes were neatly placed on the books. Then I put a folded blue and green towel beside the wall next to the blue shelf. I arranged my study books on it and used several iron clips to fix them.

There's a wood shelf on the wall beside my bed so I put some things on it. These things were my deep-colored and modern-fashioned reading lamp, a cardboard box filled with cosmetics, a long plastic tube containing tennis balls, a china brush pot containing various pens and pencils, two bottles of fashionable shampoo, and two bottles of Nestlé instant coffee and non-dairy creamer. On one end of the shelf facing the ladder by which I climbed up and down, I hung a false mouse with its tail cut off by me, presented by one of my friends. I felt a little afraid of it, so I put up a little picture of a cat behind it on the wall.

By now, as most things were in place, I began to decorate. I put a big photo album with a beautiful and romantic colored cover on the blue shelf. Just above the plastic shelf on the wall, I put up a biology-era chart and an American map, which symbolized my pursuits. A beautiful long peacock feather with its end inserted between the map and the wall increased the vividness. The most important action was to put up six portraits of some young singers and actors. To me, they were all handsome or beautiful. There is hardly any girl in our department who decorates her bed this way. But I didn't mind whether or not I did things according to others. The last thing to do was to hang the tennis racquet on the wall beside one of the portraits. When in place, it gave out much energy to the whole scene.

Several friends came to see me and appreciated the design of my little living space. I felt I had moved into a new mood.

From this experience, I find that furnishing your own room is very important. If your room is compatible with your own conceptions about beauty, and furnished to your convenience and habits of life, it becomes a real room belonging to yourself. It will make you feel comfortable and relaxed after hard work or other outside experiences.

—**Liu Jian**
Biology
SHANDONG PROVINCE

ON CAMPUS, students have next to no privacy. As Liu Jian described in her story, the students live 5 or 6 to a room in large dormitory compounds. Although there were major constructions and renovations all over campus leading up to the 1998 Centenary, I regret to say that the overcrowded dormitory compounds remained largely untouched. In the dorm there is no room for study desks or much in the way of private possessions. Students all take baths in rather squalid public bath houses. During the course of each day on campus they have little opportunity to escape from the crowds. Each day, including Sunday, as early as 6:30 A.M. to as late as 9 P.M. students compete for a good seat either in the classrooms or in the huge university library—places where it is quiet enough to do assignments or review work. Sometimes this kind of life can be difficult, as Zhou and He found out.

ONLY BECAUSE HE IS DRUNK

I went back to our dorm as usual. It appeared a little different from other days. No one spoke. No one said "Hello" to me. (They always say hello to me because of my polite attitude.) I smelt the smell of wine. Someone must be drunk.

I put away my bag and greeted them. The air in our dormitory became bitter, and I found out that Yang was drunk. He didn't drink unless he wanted to flatter someone and I knew that Yang did drink with our leader. Suddenly he spoke out, "Sun wants to kiss you." I knew it was a joke and he always make such jokes. I answered, "Close your smelly mouth."

"Shit, looking for death?" He shouted at me like a mad dog. I was also angry. "You're the son of a bitch. Who are you! Don't think that because you drink a little smelly wine, I fear you. I'm not afraid of you! Weak man." He stood up as if he wanted to beat me. I said: "Wait a minute, I don't want to interrupt others. Let's go out." We went out and had a fight. He was hurt, and my watch was broken.

I don't know who was wrong. I don't know why he acted like that to me. I was so good to him. Just three days before when he had a serious sickness, I was the person who took him to the hospital. I didn't know he was that kind of person. Maybe he is not a man, only a brute!

—**Zhou Jiantou**
Geophysics
HENAN PROVINCE

INJUSTICE

I have suffered a lot from injustice and have once made others suffer it, too, since I came to college.

When I came to Peking University, I found it hard to go to sleep. I wondered why it was that my roommates had so much energy that they played and talked long after the lights went out (till late into the night), that they seldom took naps at noon, listening instead to music, or noisily playing Chinese chess. What made it even worse was that some of them used our flat as a place for selling tiny merchandise and for renting books, so that I could not even have a rest at our flat when exhausted, because there were so many people in and out. I found no time to make up the lack of rest at all. My energy deteriorated day after day and I worried a lot about my studies. They did not care about theirs at all!

This went on for a month. Then I could not stand it any longer and told them about my discomfort. They were—and still are—very kind and told me to speak out whenever their actions interfered with me, or they would never be able to know it and make adjustments. They changed their habits a little; however, it did not help much. Thus, I began asking them to make larger changes. At last, I set up a firm timetable, according to which they were expected to go to bed before the lights were out and should not make a single sound at noon.

Several weeks passed. By this time they could not stand my "tyranny" and "rebelled." After a fierce quarrel, I bitterly realized what I had been doing and had to take naps in classrooms to prevent my energy from breaking down. It took us half a year to forgive each other completely. Our conflict ended mainly in that I gradually adapted myself to their timetable. As for them, they tried to go to bed not too late at night and to keep quiet at noon. Still, now and then they ignore me completely and then I suggest a tiny negotiation to adjust our actions. They are cooperative, while still emphasizing that their living habits ought to be respected.

I accept what they emphasize. However, my habits ought to be respected as well. I then realized that the reason why they had unbelievable energy is that they never get up early in the morning, while I do. Also, I have always been trying not to wake them up by not listening to the radio or reading the English texts aloud. I have to give up my right to do what I want to do in the morning, or they would also suffer lack of sleep! Seldom do they realize it. Since we are now living in harmony, I am not going to tell them about it.

—He Lingfeng
Chinese Department
SHANDONG PROVINCE

DESPITE SETBACKS, for most students life on campus can be very fulfilling particularly as there are many activities outside the allocated times for study, lectures, or laboratory work. At Beida over one hundred and twenty clubs or associations exist covering such fields as natural sciences, social sciences, humanities, culture, and sports. The students join these to get in touch with society, enhance their skills, and enrich their knowledge. One of these associations was called the Twentieth Century Club and I remember one night I was invited to speak at a forum. About 250 students listened to me bask in the sound of my own voice for one hour on the subject of education in Australia. Afterwards there were lots of questions on scholarships and whether overseas students in Australia faced prejudice in their daily lives, to which I admitted that some did, but most did not.

The next two brief essays give a sample of organized leisure activities on campus. First, Liu tells us how she conquered her fear and learned how to swim

LEARNING TO SWIM

I selected a swimming course as my physical education at the beginning of this semester. Though the teacher warned us of the difficulties we would come across, I was still optimistic. When I jumped into the cold water for the first time, I realized that the teacher was right. If I stopped moving for a while, I would shiver. This forced me to keep moving.

Most of my classmates had already learned to swim, while I hadn't, so I had to start by learning to float. I was afraid that the water would come into my eyes, ears, and nose. Closing my eyes and holding my breath, I put my head into the water rapidly. Fortunately I floated up easily. This encouraged me and I soon began doing leg exercises. When I saw the bottom of the swimming pool sliding backward underneath my body, I became very excited and self-confident.

By and by, I came to the period of breathing exercises. After several practice sessions, I found that I could raise my head out of the water, but couldn't breath in the air for fear of being choked by the water. One day, I didn't go to class and one of my classmates told the teacher that I could swim for 25 meters. It made me so anxious that I went swimming by myself an additional three times. I encouraged myself to try breathing and I succeeded!

Now I can swim freely. I'm proud of myself. I've recognized that I have to deal with many difficulties before gaining some achievements. It requires courage and tenacity.

—Liu Jian
Political Science
INNER MONGOLIA AUTONOMOUS REGION

IN AUSTRALIA all kids of elementary school age, myself included, learned to swim so I found Liu's story curious. I asked her for more details. I told her that in my country girls as well as boys learned to swim at an early age. She listened and told me that most Chinese boys knew how to swim and when she was a girl, her brother and boy cousins learned to swim. But I was not attuned to what she wanted to imply. You see, I was ignorant of the central place of modesty in Chinese culture and customs. So I persisted. I wanted to know why young Chinese girls didn't learn how to swim. I told Liu it seemed unfair. She struggled for the words to explain and then finally found an exquisite phrase. "In China we are more traditional. Women and girls don't open their clothes in public."

A UNIVERSITY MOUNTAINEERING TEAM

"Our team is the first university mountaineering squad in China. We lack both funds and equipment as well as coaches, but we make do with what is available and trust that our enthusiasm, hard work, and unity will tide us over all difficulties," said Xie Ruxiang, the captain of the Peking University Mountaineering Team (PUMT).

The idea to establish a mountaineering team originated during the spring of 1989. At that time Professor Cui Zhijiu, a glacier specialist and veteran mountaineer, gave a lecture on mountaineering and pointed to the ignorance of the sport in China. Some of the students present were so impressed by the lecture that they decided to form a mountaineering team as a way to stimulate Chinese interest in this sport. And before long, the PUMT was set up.

The PUMT does regular training, such as rock-climbing and camping, on the outskirts of Beijing. In winter holidays, they often go to the Heilongtan Reservoir and do some training in a snow and ice environment. With the aid of the China Mountaineering Association, they have successfully scaled four snow mountains in Northwest China. Newspapers carried detailed accounts of their achievements.

Their success and stories have met with accolades on campus. The students of neighboring Tsinghua University set up their scientific expedition association recently, with the help of the PUMT. The PUMT hopes that more and more people in China come to like mountaineering.

—**Cao Aoneng**
Probability and Statistics
HEBEI PROVINCE

SOME STUDENTS WOULD PREFER that daily life on campus reflected life in the ideal rather than life as it really is. In the next story, Bian pleads for a more modest existence among students, an existence in which differences in family wealth are concealed. But China is changing. As its economy improves people are paying more and more attention to diet and self-image. Official statistics suggest that Chinese people now spend ten times more on cosmetics than they did ten years ago. The number of beauty parlors has increased in a decade from about 10,000 to over 750,000, and the number employed in them from about 100,000 to over one million! Bian's pleas are in vain. The consumer society is no longer at the campus gates. It is now within.

THE CONSUMER SOCIETY ON CAMPUS

As the development of the outer society is marvelous, the consumption level on campus is accordingly marvelous. Compared with that of ten years ago it's really unthinkable. We can see it in the clothes people wear.

Ten years ago, there was rarely any differences between the clothes students wore, whether in color or in style. But now, if I choose any three people, what they are wearing is sure to be different. Moreover, the quality of the clothes is not the same. One is ordinary, another is a little better and the third might be altogether too magnificent.

Some people may think it's insignificant to discuss such problems, and they might say its just natural with the development of the society. But I think we should reflect on it carefully. Yes, of course the society is increasing with marvelous speed, but what about the students themselves? We are still consumers, not producers. We can't depend on ourselves yet. We still depend on our parents. As for the financial situation of us students, there should be no difference and can't be any difference if help is disregarded. We are just studying and have not begun to produce for society. When that time comes, of course ability can be distinguished and can bring in different revenue. Some students are living life ahead of their time. We can say this is a disgrace.

So I'd like to say, as students, we should lead a modest life. It's nothing to do with your family's condition, however rich or poor. Just by this way, we should and can form good habits. It's true that in the society there are some poor consumption ideas, but such ideas should not belong to our modern college students. We college students can become important people in future society. If we can't form independent habits now, when we enter society we will still not be independent.

—Bian Jie
Japanese Language
HEBEI PROVINCE

The tedium of lectures sometimes affects students. As there are times in all our lives when daily routines become almost unbearable and we yearn to escape from them, we can identify with the feelings of Wang Han, in the next imaginative story.

LECTURES, WHY ARE THERE LECTURES?

He decided on a walk. "Walk out!" He said to himself the word OUT several times, the pronunciation of which cleared his throat. He half-heartedly sought for an excuse to prove the infeasibility or the insanity of such a proposal and failed to find it, happily. For the present time, he was absolutely free: not urgently engaged, nor appointed, nor supervised by anybody. He was all alone in his room which he shared with four men, from whose presence he was free now. He could sing or cry or even scream if he chose. But he didn't, instead he went to the windowsill. Down in the road there was the crowd: hustling, rushing, streaming. He could almost feel the snatch of it even behind the defense of the panes. How great was the collective force of the actions of people to ascend to that height and for him to remain in its sway. He sighed and nearly gave in, when the stream thinned, and two cyclists collided with a BANG.

He recovered immediately from the instant quiver of indecision and left the window.

He shouldered open the door, slipped out, and backed it to prevent it from swinging. It was a little sulky in the sky and the air was damp and raw. The distance was a grayish muffled sight. Near the dorm, dried stumps and sawed-off roots were scattered recklessly about the trees. He stepped unto the road, hands in pockets. The traffic was still busy in the campus thoroughfare as it was time for afternoon lectures. He had got his own, which had been dull and useless since the very beginning, and which he had been attending too, but refused to do this time. Suddenly he realized his absolute freedom; how could he bear the thought of being preached to, with the purpose of the sermon itself but futile? He just continued. But bicycles whistled by him incessantly, stirring the air about him, making it more difficult for him to keep warm. They even click-clacked. The noises made seemed to harmonize in an enchanting symphony, which had odd effects on him. But he went on anyhow.

They were model students, thought he; they all looked attentive, diligent, and severe, concentrating on the control of their vehicles, as on the control of themselves. Are they, controlled and controlling, free? This he knew not. An uneasiness caught him which he felt a sickness in defining. Not as justified as before, he slackened his steps, slowed down and, at last, stopped to watch. A cyclist rode towards the human stream, fighting his way, extracting a few curses and hateful stares on the part of those in the way. "FREAK!" The word came to his mind as the bike finally maneuvered through and passed by him. Then he heard a crash. Am I walking out or just freaking out? He began to feel a restlessness in his stomach, which he walked on to ease.

The thoroughfare turned acutely. A huge traffic mirror was set upon the acme of the angle. He paused. Bicycles whistled by as before. He looked into the glass at himself and found strangely enough, distorted in both shape and proportion, his face got twice fuller, occupying more than one third of the whole reflected human being. He studied this comic image of himself with much curiosity. Such a big, idiotic head and such tiny, dwarfish limbs! How impotent were actions compared with the thoughts that had initiated them! He stood and mused until the sting of the cold wind awoke him. He came to and strode away, making his way towards the classroom building.

It's a quarter past two, not too late yet.

—Wang Han
Guanghua School of Management
GANSU PROVINCE

UNLIKE THEIR PARENTS and grandparents, for the post-Mao generation there is no guarantee of secure employment once they graduate—the days of the "iron rice bowl" are gone. Although all my undergraduates were full-time students and all of the same age group, more and more of them sought opportunities to earn money through tutoring or other part-time work. More and more in today's China, they need money to pay for living expenses and increasingly costly tuition.

In the next story Li Na provides her thoughts on the necessity and the benefits of working while studying.

IS IT GOOD FOR COLLEGE STUDENTS TO HAVE PART-TIME JOBS?

Nowadays more and more college students go out into society to find jobs. About ten years ago, college students spent most of their time studying and reading in the library. But now, with the rapid advancement of the Chinese economy and improvement in the Chinese people's economic consciousness, doing business has flourished. This also influences the campus. Modern students become less bookish. Attracted by the world outside, they try entering society to do part-time jobs.

These part-time jobs vary. Some of them act as home tutors of middle-school students. Some find jobs in companies, others are assistants in grocery stores or sell Christmas cards, coats, tapes, or some electronic appliances. Reasons for having part-time jobs vary too.

First of all, students who have part-time jobs can relieve, to some extent, the economic burdens of their families or parents. Frankly speaking, life in college now is not so easy as what it was in the old days. Prices go up every day, while the state only allots 49 yuan a month to an undergraduate student. But the average food cost adds up to about 200 yuan a month! Parents feed their college sons and daughters. It seems shameful to ask parents for money after the age of 20, especially with such a proud name—a student in Peking University. After all, when my father was at the same age, he was able to support the whole family! Nowadays college people are pursuing something different—romance, maturity, independence or brilliant academic records. Being able to earn their own money gives students a feeling that they've become adults and, therefore, makes them feel more mature.

As I have said, some of the students teach pupils as part-time tutors. Since college students all get very high marks in entrance exams, it is easy for them to teach what they have learned. A student can't make big bucks in this way, but it's enough for a student and better than going to a disco at weekends or chasing a girl by sending gifts. From another angle, after-school jobs teach those from rich families how hard it is to earn money and helps develop thriftiness in the younger generation.

Second, to have part-time jobs is like enrolling oneself in another class to learn different but necessary things. A part-time job helps cultivate independence and also fosters a sense of competition. Students have no "iron rice bowls" any more.

If one works in a company, one should know how to deal with one's workmates and the boss. Different environments need different ways of solving problems. In a university, one can finish a degree all by one's own efforts without the help from one's classmates. But in society, no one can finish tasks without the cooperation of the group one works in. Part-time jobs can be good for students' personal development. Students lead a routine life in a space bound by classrooms, dorms and cafes. It is so boring for breezy pre-adults. Life without new experiences is terrible. The future needs well-educated people, not narrow-minded bookworms. So, part-time jobs open the door to the colorful and complicated world awaiting the college students.

Besides the two reasons above, there's still another sound one. Some bright college students also try to find part-time jobs, for they did not wish to waste time studying something either useless or uninteresting, or sitting in their warm dorms and chatting for hours about trifles. One always has several decisions to make and sometimes one needs to make very careful choices. But before making them one should know what he (she) really wants to do and in which area he (she) can achieve the most. Only careful selections can help one find the best position in life.

I worked as a part-time assistant both at the 8th Far East & Pacific Sports Games for the Disabled and later at an international conference. Through my working experience I gained new energy to throw my efforts into computer programming and continue my goal of mastering English. So, when I went back to my studies, my targets were clearer, and I studied happily and confidently, for I knew what I was working for.

—**Li Na**
Computing
HAINAN PROVINCE

ALTHOUGH LIFE AS A TEACHER on campus was never dull, once the strangeness and novelty of teaching in China had worn off and my classes were used to the work routines, I noticed the students sometimes had low energy levels. One of my more experienced foreign expert friends, a Canadian who had taught in China for several years, said that quite often this was caused by overwork and poor food. So I decided to make allowances, I needed to be more relaxed in class, to just talk more to the students, to tell them stories and draw them out.

To give the students more opportunity for talking English I arranged an English Corner every week in my apartment. When the students came, some just listened, some merely asked polite questions about my family and the weather in Australia. Others wanted to know more about drugs, girlfriends and boyfriends, the generation gap, and human rights. Others wanted fatherly advice on

Compulsion

how to cope with loneliness on campus, or how to find a friend.

One day in class I noticed the students were in a fever of excitement because they had been asked to give blood. Apparently they all had to do so, unless they had exemption on health grounds. Their compensation was a small monetary payment. Wild talk circulated about the huge quantities of blood being taken and the horrendous after-effects. Some said it would cause exhaustion for weeks and be extremely painful. Others claimed blood types betrayed your personality characteristics and foretold your future life.

I found the talk endearing and familiar, but at a deeper level the talk was disturbing because it triggered something. It led me to the need to acknowledge an attitude I had towards China. A somewhat shameful attitude perhaps. But I need to admit it.

The talk was endearing because these Chinese 20 year-olds were no different from students that I was familiar with from my own society. It was endearing because the young people back home had the same bubbles of tension when preparing to give blood and, afterwards, explosions of relief when talking among their peers about their experiences. Yet, it was disturbing because I knew blood screening techniques and hygiene practices in China could not match those in Australia. In fact, I had been advised by the Australian Embassy doctor to avoid blood transfusions in China. Yes, I was becoming more accustomed to life in China, but I knew I could never become fully acclimated, I could never put my body on the line. I was glad I had a passport out of China. I prayed that, if it became a matter of life and death, I would not have to rely on Chinese medical services.

The Great Learning

When we were too young to form our own opinion, we regarded what a teacher said as truth without questioning. Now, as university students, sometimes we don't go in the footprint of teachers. We have begun to realize that they are human and can make mistakes.

It is sad, even a shame, to think no one from China (which often boasts that people here are the most intelligent) has won the Nobel Prize; whereas small Taiwan has two! There are big problems in the Chinese education system without doubt. We need to be more independent: if we just follow our teachers without questioning, everyone will have some unknown weaknesses.

—**Zhang Bin** ◆ *Mathematics* ◆ ZHEJIANG PROVINCE

ONE PLEASANT SURPRISE in adjusting to the rhythm of living on a campus in China was the release from the pressure of bureaucratic work. A great deal of that pressure back in Australia had been exciting and creative, but not all of it. In Beijing there were no more days bursting with meetings and deadlines piled on deadlines. No more crazy telephone calls about urgent requests or minor crises in response to political twists and turns of the day. Working days in Beijing were so unlike those occasional "bad days" in Canberra, and I did not miss that part of my past. Here I had little to do with the day-to-day administration; my Chinese colleagues were pleased to see me, and were grateful for my efforts. But they and the students, let's face it, could survive without me.

It was peculiar to have so much free time for myself, both at work and afterwards. It was peculiar too, after twenty-eight years, to have no family to go home to and share the events and feelings of the day. Although I found it easy to become absorbed in my own world it was sometimes a little too monastic. I missed the in-depth comment on current affairs, the alternative voice in the public forum, the margin for dissent. Part of this was due to my ignorance of the Chinese language.

As knowing some Chinese was necessary for survival and self-respect, I tried in my spare time to build on the slender foundations begun in Australia. After work during 1992 and 1993, two days each week, I had attended the Canberra Institute of Technology evening classes in Mandarin. In Beijing, four times a week, I attempted to improve my Chinese a little by exchanging one hour of English for one hour of Chinese. It was a stimulating experience as each of my Chinese tutors had very different backgrounds. One was a medical research scientist, originally from a very poor village in Shanxi Province, two were graduate students, but raised in small towns in Hunan and Jiangsu, and the last was a bright undergraduate from Tianjin with a wonderful knowledge of old China.

This gentle act of self-discipline, that is, struggling to learn Chinese, served as a reminder of just how advanced my students had become through their study of English at school over twelve or more years. Almost every Chinese student takes English while at secondary school, and, as far as I could tell, all university students study it too. Admittedly, most of them could not speak articulately or translate spoken English quickly in their heads due to lack of exposure to native speakers. But why were they so keen to improve their understanding of written English? This dedication to recognizing written English was for the most practical of reasons, as I was to find out.

During the winter vacation at the end of my first year of teaching, I had the opportunity to get out of freezing Beijing. So I visited the cities of Shaoxing, Shanghai and Nanjing. These places are within several hundred kilometers of one another in central eastern China. This opportunity arose because I had been invited to the famous Shanghai High School to teach English to some senior school administrators for five weeks.

On the way to Shanghai, I visited several universities including the University of the South East, a huge technological institute in Nanjing where Ming Hongwei, brother of one of my Chinese-Australian friends, was Dean of the Electrical Engineering Department. Although Hong Wei's spoken English was rudimentary, we managed to communicate through a mixture of my terrible Chinese, his English, and much goodwill. He proudly showed me through his engineering building, especially a center containing state-of-the-art engineering equipment. At that time some graduate students were busy working there. Three were on Internet receiving or transmitting technical engineering messages; another was using an advanced software package containing multicolored high-resolution 3-D images of integrated circuits. None of them could speak to me in English. Nevertheless, they were all communicating in English through the computer. Like my students at Beida, they knew the importance of absorbing the essentials of the language of the Information Age: English.

One of my close friends, Zhang Meihua, was a Vice-Chairman in the English Department. One day when we were talking about education, she gave me her general opinion about the students at Beida—the post-

Mao generation. It was a rather gloomy view and one I did not share with her. She said that Chinese youth were now without roots or ideals. Sometimes I saw this kind of fear reflected in English-language newspapers in China. For example, a *China Daily* editorial in October 1995 commented on the fact that, as a result of the imposition of the one-child policy in 1979, over sixty percent of the 1995 intake of university students was from one-child families, and this percentage would rise in future years. The editorial was concerned that this was a self-centered generation pampered by parents and caring little about other people:

> The common fear in the country is that this generation may not be able to sacrifice for others, let alone society. Students should learn to live with other people, work in teams, be conscious of their community and, moreover, be persons who can and would like to do something for others instead of always taking from society.

Perhaps more so than in Australia and elsewhere in the West, in China students have a high status, for they embody learning and responsibility. Yet, the concepts of education and knowledge seem a little different here. There is not the same expectation that knowledge in one field ought to include interconnectivity to other knowledge, and that, if understood at sufficient depth, one aspect of knowledge ought to lead to wider understanding. The enormous amount of rote learning of Chinese characters in early schooling has something to do with this, as does the now defunct Confucian tradition of much classical learning for admission by examination to official positions in the service of the emperor. In Chinese education there seems to be much more memory work, more detailed information carefully packaged for the students to remember and repeat. The expectation seems to be that at university the student will go deeper and narrower, thus becoming more specialized.

In my first English classes, I found the students waiting for me to give them information so that they could dutifully repeat it later. I fought this expectation. I told them I had no information to give them, that my job was to improve their skills. It took a few lessons before they realized that I meant what I said.

Of course Chinese students are just as pragmatic as university students in Australia or elsewhere—as pragmatic as I was as a student. That is, most of them know what they want and know what the system wants. They know that the quickest way to personal success is by delivering, not questioning.

A young architect Cai Chixi, whom I met in Shanghai, is an example of this kind of realism. Cai, who was in his late twenties, claimed he already owned two apartments in Shanghai; he was intent on making a fortune. He asked me whether I knew how long it took to obtain a Masters Degree in Architecture in New Zealand. I said, if all the necessary prerequisites had been fulfilled, it usually takes two years. I asked him why New Zealand, and he said this was the quickest way he knew to gain the necessary qualifications for registration as an architect in Shanghai. He needed the registration to cash in on the building boom.

However, in China as elsewhere, not all students are so utilitarian as Cai. Some students expect deeper, more lasting outcomes from education, as was the case with Xu Dongsheng, who later was to continue as a graduate student at Beida:

TO BE FREE THROUGH EDUCATION

Somewhere or other the American author Irving Stone once said that only through education can a man be free and rise in this world. I took it for granted and thought that just doing or not doing study made the difference. With time going by, I realized that it is also a matter of how to do it, in other words, how should I be educated to develop myself.

Before I entered the university, it never occurred to me that what school taught me was not necessarily what I needed to take in. I discovered that what I should know could not be obtained entirely through curricula at school. For a long time I did what I was told, which is far from the right way to study. Anyway, to enter Peking University I had no choice but to stick to the strict pattern of education of that time.

However after a year as a freshman, I find to my disappointment that I can't take in all of what professors pour on us, yet I did it pretty well at school. Even though I'm more studious, the poor grades seemed to bear out that old pitiful saying, "The more I learn, the less I know."

Tired, frustrated and more puzzled, I can't help asking myself where on earth my study methods went wrong? Maybe it is my attitude, on which all my methods are based—an attitude that does not fit into college study. Then I begin to doubt the validity of absorbing all the information given to me and later giving it back to the professors on exam papers to verify that I've been well educated. Undoubtedly in doing so I'll pull straight A's, given time and dedication. So what? Sitting through four years of instruction and doing nothing else. Small wonder, I'll become a container of lists of equations and principles.

Through this kind of education will I be free or rise in the world? What a daydream!

Now, what does being well-educated really mean? To be skillful and qualified, I think, is the first stage. Then it means to be learned and capable. But it also means to be wise enough to live a free life, full of contentment and truth, satisfying the mind, appealing to the heart, firing the will.

However, age does not go hand in hand with wisdom, nor does education. The current mass-education system includes everyone, but is not the best way to educate each individual. So, to reach the highest stage, to be wise and free, I must also try other ways. Nobody can do it for me, and I have no idea of how to do it without trying. The only thing I'm sure of is to do it through self-education, which means I keep an active role in the process. I plan for myself instead of following the prevailing route without thought. I find and accept what I need instead of receiving what I'm offered. I test my abilities and wisdom instead of being pressed down or cheered up only by exams and grades. So, the education I'm now taking is an education on my terms.

With this attitude, I can draw out my own methods. In short, to be active in studying I decide what I need and lack, then go for the answer. I try to solve it with my acquired knowledge. In most cases, it may be beyond me, but only where there is a challenge followed by a response will there be an improvement.

Xu Dongsheng
Geophysics
TIANJIN

EDUCATION has a central position in Chinese Government policy. There are a number of legislative measures in force to maintain a national system which attempts to retain sufficient flexibility to adapt to local conditions and needs. Education, whether at the university or primary level, receives inadequate funding. Although the situation has improved (for example in 1949 university graduates were about 0.1% of the population and now they are approaching 3.0%), the government is not spending enough on its schools, technical institutes and universities.

If adult learning institutions are included, there are about 2,200 universities in China. Yet, too many of them are sub-standard, and many are no more than single purpose vocational institutions; universities in name only. The government has begun the process of choosing 100 of the best as key universities to help China compete on the world stage. Considerable reforms are now afoot, with the government planning to maintain macro-economic control while giving universities greater power to make their own decisions. When all the bureaucratic euphemisms are stripped away what this means in practice is that universities need to raise more money to survive. As a consequence, many universities, including Beida, have abolished free tuition.

More and more university students aspire to attend overseas universities, especially in the United States of America where there are already more Chinese students than from any other nation. At Beida, for example, about one in ten go abroad soon after graduation. Many don't come back, at least in the short term. This does not help China, which, already short of technical and professional expertise, is unlikely to have a sufficient supply early next century to meet new scientific and technological demands.

In the next brief essay Dong Yiyang expresses his views on university education.

A VIEW ON CHINA'S UNIVERSITY EDUCATION

My mother did not receive a University education because of illness. As a result, she had to struggle for a job for many years while her classmates who entered colleges easily got one.

In those days in China, if you managed to go to college your life became very different. The need for highly educated people was so great that the government paid for senior education and provided the students with three meals a day and money. All had been arranged by the government. These lucky young people did not need to worry about the future. After graduation, each would be offered a job according to the demands of government. The other people of the same age, who were not so lucky, were forced into factories, shops or farms to make a living.

My mother, as one of those unlucky people, had a mind that her children should get senior education. She often described how good campus life was to us. "Everything is well arranged," she said. "Just study and play. You do not need to worry about the future." The campus sounded like heaven. I never doubted that I would go to college.

In September 1994 I entered the campus of the Peking University and I began to find out that the campus was not the heaven my mother described. With the development of the society, the economy, and education in China, campus life was changed greatly and differed very much from that of the old days.

First, the function of college education has changed. In the past, an individual was considered as "a screw in a machine," which meant people were just laborers of the country and personal feelings were hardly taken into account. The government only regarded the students as the more educated laborers, who could contribute more to government plans than the others. Now however, more emphasis is placed on personal development. We receive college education mainly to make ourselves grow.

Second, the gaining of knowledge changes. In the past, a student only learned the courses of his own department, to be what the government wanted him to be. Then, most students worked very hard, wanting A's. Now we never stop learning and poring over books. But we care less about the courses of our own departments. For us, knowledge is power. This is especially true in a market economy.

Third, campus life becomes harder than before. As I outlined above, in the past, the government paid for education and provided the students three meals a day and money. However now, not only has the function of senior education changed, but also the government cannot afford the increasing tuition costs. Students must pay for their university education. Tuition is usually more than 1,000 yuan a year, which is a large amount of money for most of China's families. To our delight, some measures have been taken to help the poor students.

My campus life will be precious for me. Though the campus is not heaven, it is a school that teaches me many things. During these years at the Peking University, I develop myself in many ways. I will tell others about campus life with great honor.

Dong Yiyang
Probability and Statistics
ANHUI PROVINCE

IN CHINA there is much dissatisfaction with the pressing necessity for schools to supplement their inadequate public sector income with profits from business ventures and donations from parents or benefactors. As I could see from visits to secondary schools in Kunming, Shijiazhuang, Wuhan, Shaoxing, Tianjin, Shanghai, and other small and large cities, this need led to unfair practices such as special places in preferred schools for children of parents with influence or money. It also tended to increase the gap in educational opportunities: the better schools improve their facilities even further and increase their funds for teaching bonuses and other incentives.

Here is an example of what I mean. Shanghai High School, at which I taught during my first winter vacation, is a distinguished scholarship school to which Chinese students are admitted on merit. About 10 percent of the students were not scholarship holders but 'observer' students admitted on the basis of their parents support for the school. It also contained a small international senior school charging high fees. Inside the spacious school grounds were several profit-making ventures which added considerably to the school's income. The school grounds and teaching facilities were at least equal to those of better comprehensive high schools I was familiar with in Australia. The library was superior, as the books and the building had been donated by an overseas Chinese businessman. Tuition fees were not charged but some of the boarding costs needed to be met by parents, except those of very poor students.

I arrived at Shanghai High School just before the end of the school semester. On the day after my arrival parents came to take children (and their possessions) home for winter holidays. To do this almost every kind of vehicle was used, including handcarts, bicycles, taxis, corporate owned vehicles, and a surprising number of huge American luxury cars. About one kilometer away was the district high school for this overpopulated, struggling suburban area of Shanghai. The contrast between the two schools could not have been more marked. An American luxury car had probably never entered the place; it was overcrowded, cramped, and poorly equipped.

Du Mei's story, which follows, reflects the unease with which the need for schools to raise money is viewed by most Chinese people.

THE FUNCTION OF SCHOOLS

It is well-known that the teachers are the spirit engineers of human beings and books are the stepping stones for human development. At Peking University we all want to be outstanding people, and the society needs this, too. So, we must learn a lot of things throughout our lives by all kinds of means. But we usually learn most knowledge, especially the most basic and important, from books and teachers at college and schools. Then what on earth is the function of colleges and schools? It is to provide excellent professors and abundant books, supply excellent facilities and create an active academic atmosphere. In short, the function is just to teach.

Is the status quo really like this? Do teachers really try their best to teach students? I don't know.

With the market economy written into our constitution, all the enterprises and individuals begin to push themselves into the market. They pursue profit and chase wealth. This is not wrong. But, colleges and schools aren't willing to be the exception. They divert their attention to participating in market competition, setting up companies and trying to attain great profit.

We can't deny our China is short of funds for education. In order to get money to improve teaching levels, the schools should take some measures to build more financial resources. However, we must not forget what should be the center of our attention. We should focus on teaching, not profit. We mustn't forget the function of schools. It's our social duty. At the same time, it's our honor, too.

Du Mei
International Politics
HUBEI PROVINCE

AT BEIDA, students are admitted to either science or humanities disciplines on the basis of their high school scores in the annual National Examinations. Some particularly bright students are admitted without examination. Only these students and those who score highest on the exams have the freedom to choose their own major. All others are assigned a major about which, sometimes, they know nothing. Such was the case with Li Qian, the son of a poor schoolmaster from a small city in Sichuan. Much to his dismay, Li discovers he has been assigned to study Urdu.

WHO THE HELL SPEAKS URDU

August 24th, 1994 found me dumbfounded after receiving an admission slip from the Department of Oriental Languages of Peking University. "Shit!" I even didn't know whom to cuss at." "Damn those sons of bitches…"

I had just heard the name Urdu for the first time in my life at that very moment through the damn notification. "Who the hell speaks such a language of which I even don't know a single word?" I thought in madness.

But life didn't go mad, it is always so impersonal, and everybody has to face up to it. In China, an ordinary graduate of a high school can do nothing but obey the notification from any University or college, if he wants to go to college at all. Being a 16-year-old son of a poor teacher of a country school, definitely I wasn't in the position to do otherwise. I hadn't the power. So I just did as I had been told.

After a year's training in the army, I came to this campus. Soon I learned that Urdu was a native language spoken in Pakistan and that most of its letters came from Arabic while its pronunciation was awfully similar to that of Hindi. Moreover, many of its words derived from Persian. Just a mess! And instead of left to right, every line of Urdu begins at the right. What a thing! But I had to do well in it, even though I didn't like it. It's my habit to do everything as well as possible. Above all, I had to specialize in it, and just because very few Chinese knew it, it might help me find a decent job. So I tried my best to recite every new word slipping from the teacher's tongue.

Now I'm in grade two. Looking back, I find I spent too much time in studying Urdu and I need to learn other things. So I've been working hard at English this term. Of course, pronunciation is still a problem for me and the fact that I come from a high school located in a remote place of Sichuan makes it more difficult. Maybe I can do better in writing or listening, but I always feel at a loss with oral exercises. But, mind you, I have the confidence to learn English better and better, and I don't think I would ever be frustrated. Never.

Undoubtedly I'm not just a bookworm without any thoughts or dreams. In fact, I always think about where to go and what to do after graduation, though there is still one and a half years left. There is a likelihood that I may work with Urdu for at least a period, since it's difficult for me to abandon anything I've paid so much attention to. In that case, there will still be alternatives for me to choose from. One way is that I can work in an important ministry of government or serve as employee in some company. The former is an important position and the latter can bring much more money—but I don't like to work too early.

Another method is that I can continue my study to M.A. or even Ph.D. But in China, even the best Urdu teachers, who are all in our campus, are not competent to supervise an M. A., for none of them is an M.A. or Ph.D. So my dream is to study Urdu further in one of those most famous universities abroad which are known for researching Urdu. And there are still many such dreams in my heart. In short, if I want to use Urdu, first I should master it.

Obviously, being a 20 year-old college kid, I haven't enough insight to foresee clearly what I will be in future, for I'm so green. But I'm still optimistic about my prospects. After all, I'm working hard, and I have the confidence as well as the time.

Li Qian
Urdu Language
SICHUAN PROVINCE

A CREDIT SYSTEM enables Beida students to select minor courses, provided they fulfill requirements for majors. For undergraduates the annual pass rates and graduation rates are much higher than in Australian universities—over 90% compared with some 70% in Australia. Many students are interested in postgraduate opportunities, and postgraduate entry is via examination. However, some students are recommended for postgraduate study on the basis of their academic achievement and good character.

Economics and Law are the most prestigious disciplines. Through economics and related disciplines students can aspire to business careers and high salaries. Law graduates are in very high demand too as China needs many more lawyers to successfully negotiate with foreign firms and handle increasingly complex legal matters. In addition, Beida has excellent computing, physical science and life science courses. Zhou Henghui, in the next extract, talks about his major, Biology, and its importance to the modern world.

BIOLOGY TODAY

If you eat some kinds of oranges, you may realize that they have no seeds; if you go out into the fields, you may wonder why some crops thrive without insecticides. That's due to the development of modern biology.

Though human beings have existed in the world for thousands of years, it was not until the middle of this century that we began to know the answers as to why we resemble our parents. Watson and Crick, very famous biologists and Nobel Prize winners, discovered the structure of DNA, which became the foundation of modern biology. They explained how this complex information is passed on from generation to generation. And now biologists are trying to unravel the complete genetic code of human beings and to set up banks of "genetic fingerprints."

Living things are quite different from non-living objects. Life has its own variety, complexity and efficiency and the nature of life is our great teacher. Men invented the solar battery, but men cannot use solar energy as efficiently as a small grass plant does in its photosynthesis process. With more biological knowledge, we can make such wonders ourselves. Now, biologists can duplicate some plants. That is, they can make some cells taken from them (but not seeds) grow into a full plant which is exactly the same. Using this technique, we can produce crops of high quality.

Biology has become an applied science. Biologists are doing experimental research of vaccines for drugs to prevent widespread damage from heart attacks. Farmers also benefit from biotechnology. They suffer less from chemical fertilizer, because biologists help them to choose, even to create the kind of crop to fit the weather and the soil.

New biology means more energy and more harvests. Biologists work hard for a better world for the entire human race.

Zhou Henghui
Biology
HUNAN PROVINCE

MEDICINE, whether Western or Chinese, is of lower prestige than in Western countries. Doctors are often poorly paid and medicine is seen as a high stress, high health risk job. Nevertheless, very good students still choose Medicine and for the most admirable of reasons. Such students often undertake biological science at a university like Beida before proceeding to a medical university, as was the case with Wu Chun.

WHY I CHOSE TO BE A DOCTOR

I can clearly remember the very day when I decided to enroll at Peking Union Medical College. It was a hot summer's day, just after my schoolmates and I had finished the college entrance examination. Although exhausted by hard work in those three days, I was still excited. All the efforts I had made would be paid back soon. I scanned through the advertisements of all kinds of colleges which were pasted on the board. Famous names jumped before my eyes one by one. Peking University which attracted me from my childhood, Tsinghua University, Zhejiang University, and so on, all seemed to wave their hands at me. Finally I got to the name I desired: Peking Union Medical College. Its advertisement was not well-decorated, but a red cross in the middle of it drew my attention at once. And I knew I had got what I wanted and I also knew what I was confronted with: I had to take another eight years of study courses, the first three of which were to be in the Biology Department of Peking University.

My friends were all surprised. They kept questioning me. Why didn't I choose another major because of my high score? They thought economics was the best choice because the economy of our country was developing fast and the graduates from Economics Institutes were better paid than doctors in China. I knew it very well, too. But I couldn't betray the belief I had held from my youth.

My mother was once a physician in a country hospital. And I grew up in the hospital where my mother worked. Because my mother was always busy, I often wandered alone in the hospital building. All the things there seemed strange and odd to me. The walls were painted white, people were dressed in white and even their faces were pale too. The place was filled with a terrible smell which often made me feel sick. And its quietness often forced me to run out of it, full of fear.

When I grew up a little, I began realize another side of the hospital. Beneath the quietness lay hope—hope from the patients, from their relatives, and from the unselfish devotion of doctors and nurses. I got that idea from my mother. She seldom stayed at home. Even on Sundays, her rest was interrupted by urgent calls from the hospital. Every time she told us not to wait for her and was not back till midnight. I couldn't understand why my mother worked so hard until I read some of the letters from the patients my mother cured. In their letters, they showed their high respect for my mother's ability and her care. So I knew why mother spent all her time with her patients and I was deeply moved, for by then my mother was in very bad health. Now my mother has been retired from the hospital for two years. But her patients don't forget her. My mother usually receives New Year's gifts from them.

I now wish to carry on my mother's career. Certainly, it's a difficult and long way to go and I will need to give greater effort than other guys do. But what I learn today will be a powerful weapon with which I can fight for the better health of people. To be a competent and dedicated doctor is not as easy as talking about it. I am on the way now and I believe that I can reach my destination.

Wu Chun
Biology
HUBEI PROVINCE

EVEN AT BEIDA, for some academic faculties, such as Classical Chinese Literature, raising money through related business ventures is not easy and there is a real struggle for survival. As Dong Hong tells us, Chinese Literature is not a popular choice among the students because of limited job prospects and careers.

ABOUT CHINESE LITERATURE

The Chinese Department of Peking University used to be the most adored place for social sciences students. But now in modern society, with the development of the economy, people's ideas have changed. So, the Chinese Department is confronted with a great problem. A lot of people can't tolerate a poverty-stricken life so that they abandon their warm-heartedness towards studying Chinese Literature.

In fact, there is still a long way for us to go to study Chinese Literature. On the one hand, Chinese Literature has abundant substance, China being one of the most well-known civilizations of long standing in the world. So, there are some good traditions for us to carry on and further develop. On the other hand, in the open age, the cultural exchanges are more and more frequent. Chinese Literature is not just useful in China, but is also important when contacting foreign cultures. So there is much work to do to promote mutual understanding and friendship between Chinese and the peoples of other countries.

Such things are easier to say than to do. We must make a lot of effort to give full play to Chinese Literature. Of the students, the most important things are twofold. One is to learn the basic knowledge about literature, the classical and the popular. The second is to make progress in foreign languages, especially English, which is the best bridge to facilitate the flow of culture between China and other countries. All this comes down to making the world understand China and making China understand the world.

As for me, the reason why I choose this major is purely out of interest. At first, I think there is much pleasure in literature. But now, I have realized that there is still a long way for me to go to enter the world of literature. It will only be after hard efforts that I will claim proudly that my specialty is Chinese Literature.

Dong Hong
Chinese Department
GUIZHOU PROVINCE

ACADEMICS IN CHINA are very poorly paid. Unlike Australian academics, my Chinese colleagues lack both industrial muscle and tried and true industrial relations mechanisms to improve their salaries and conditions. In addition, compared with Australian universities, there is not the same freedom of movement within the system for academics, at least those I knew of in the Social Sciences and Humanities, to encourage analysis and synthesis of ideas, pursuit of individual thought, or to dissent. On the up side, inasmuch as I could judge, their behavior as role models is exemplary. Irrespective of academic discipline, they encourage diligence, honesty and helpfulness among the students.

So, how are teachers seen through students eyes? The first two stories which follow are of teachers whose characters strongly influenced two students. In the third and fourth, two students describe how they saw me; their descriptions include a few of my more obvious shortcomings.

Portrait of a Teacher

Sitting in a small classroom at the beginning of the first semester of my junior schooling, I felt a little uneasy. I'd heard of the teacher who would be in charge of us; he was rather a strict man in the school legends.

The bell was ringing. A man came in. He was not as tall as I'd expected. I can't recall his clothes in every detail. I just have a deep impression of his big-sized trousers. There couldn't be bigger ones. They make him look a little funny. The blinking small eyes in his face quickly overwhelmed the fun. The eyes told us he was really a serious man. Besides his frozen face, what struck me most was a big wooden stick in his hand. When he came up to me, I could sense the pain it would give. He looked at me with a smile, which frightened me even more. "You will be our monitor," he said. I stood up, and saw that my classmates would not look at me. They still stared at the stick.

In class, Mr. Li, the teacher, never relaxed the mask of his face. He would often say to a mistake-making student, "Never a little carelessness in Math, it will cause big problems." The poor guy under the stick flying around over his head, promised with tears that he would not do so again. Indeed, he dared not.

After class, Mr. Li was humorous. Smiles lit on his face and he told us a lot of jokes. At that time, we loved the 10-minute break and those jokes. I asked him one day with all my courage about the stick in order to persuade him to give it up. He said still smiling, with slyness, "I picked it up casually on the first day, and happened to take it to class. It seemed to frighten all of you. So I kept it. Though I will not really use it on anyone's head, it is effective. Don't you think so?" He whispered again, "Don't tell anyone, OK!"

In the graduating semester, we were asked to choose a high school. My mother thought I'd better go to professional school as it was a risk to go to general school, when preparing for University Entrance Exams. "Ask your mother to see me." Mr. Li didn't say much more to me at the time. He did to my mother. I didn't know how hard he'd tried. At last, Mum stopped worrying about the risk I would take, and permitted me to choose a general school.

In the next three years, I studied in a high school, and left Mr. Li. During the three years, he still cared about my progress. He asked my new teacher about me now and then. He stuck to the belief I would enter a well-known college. He was right. Now, he can receive a card from Peking University every Christmas. Mr. Li is just one of those teachers who have helped with my study and life. I write about him in my essay, and I write all such teachers in my heart.

Xie Xiaopei
Geophysics
JILIN PROVINCE

THE TEACHER I WILL REMEMBER FOREVER

She was my mathematics teacher in middle school. At that time, she was well-known for her two nicknames, "Yellow Tiger" and "Huangdoupo." No one ever knew who was the inventor and what their original meaning was. Indeed, these two names were not very respectful to a teacher, and we daren't address her so to her face. But as I think back, I find there is some truth in them.

Tigers are always fearsome. We called her Yellow Tiger not because she was strong or physically related to a tiger. In fact, she was very short, no more than 1.58 meters and suffered much from illness. But she was very strict. She set high standards for us, from sanitation in our dormitories to the improvement of our study. Whenever we did something casually, she would make us try again. She seldom showered criticism on us. She had her special and effective way of just looking at us hard. Her eyes weren't big and they were often strained from lack of sleep. But once we met them in those circumstances, we knew what we must do next.

Her second nickname, Huangdoupo, was a good description of her relation with students as it means yellow bean, or food, grandmother. In spite of her family's protestation, she spent most of her time at school. At noon, she would wander about our dormitories with a food bowl in her hands. Often, her own meal would be spoiled for her effort to find lost bowls for students or make fresh dishes for sick students. As we were far away from our home, we felt the devotion of an unselfish mother.

To me, she paid special attention. Before I became her student, I was a trouble-maker in class. I quarreled not only with my desk mate, but with the teacher as well. Sometimes I knew I was wrong, but I would never admit it for I couldn't endure the speaking tone of those people. But when she came, I often felt uneasy at the sight of her. She never criticized me. But when I achieved something, the encouragement she gave me was great enough for me to go further.

I really owe a lot to this teacher. She drew a new effort out of me. From then on, I knew where I was headed and that I must go all out for it.

Xu Xiaoyan
Biochemistry
SICHUAN PROVINCE

THE FOREIGN TEACHER IN MY EYES

It was a September morning when I first saw him, Mr. Tony Gallagher, my foreign English teacher. Though I had been studying English for more than eight years, I had never had a foreign English teacher before. So, with a few nerves and also a little curiosity, I looked at him carefully. He was a tall, white, middle-aged man and wore a pair of glasses on his characteristic straight nose. When he wrote on the blackboard, I found that he was left-handed.

I can't remember how we began the class that day, but I can still clearly remember the aroused amazement when he answered our question, "What do you think about Beijing University?" With a smile he said that actually he had only been in China for a couple of weeks. "Oh," we cried, "Really?" I was somehow excited. Perhaps for him, an Australian, we, his Chinese students, were the first group of Chinese people he knew. Similarly, to some degree, for us, he represented Australians.

Mr. Gallagher teaches us Extensive Reading in English and is absolutely a responsible teacher. His class is always arranged fully and colorful. Every time we do a lot of things: extensive reading, Australian material, jokes, class exercises, and so on. Every time he gives us 10 minutes to write an essay about a certain topic which has been given in the last class and at the same time hands out the papers we turned in the last time. The essay has been already corrected when we get them again, both in grammar and in meaning. Sometimes there is an extra remark such as "original" on it. Once, I happened to have a glance at his note book and was so surprised to find that there's a list in it which is composed of our names in "Pinyin," some dates and several "tick" marks indicating who has done the class exercise of a certain day. I was so moved. Since Beida has a free atmosphere of study, teachers seldom collect homework and correct it. But this Australian does, and even has made such a complete register.

Though he is an Australian, Mr. Gallagher was born in London. So during the first few weeks, when he smiled little and often appeared with a straight face, I had associated him with the solemn British gentlemen whom I saw in films, and was a little afraid of him and felt shy to talk in English in class. But things changed soon. One morning, he told us that when he read one of the students' essays he found this piece of advice, "Please smile more often." So he decided to accept it. Then he smiled, gently and kindly. From then on, the classes became more and more lively. I could never forget his expression when he told us how tall a kangaroo was. "A big one," he measured, "is just as tall as I am." Then he smiled with a very naive expression just as a naughty boy would. And I will remember forever his encouraging words to improve my English. "What you need is to practice." Now, I feel no longer embarrassed when speaking in English in class, and sometimes I could even raise my hand to answer questions or ask him questions.

Mr. Gallagher loves his country deeply. Every time when he tells us something about Australia, his voice is full of pride and happiness. "I am an Australian. I come from Australia." He always says this proudly. In his little comfortable apartment in North Guest House, there are things of Australia everywhere—maps, pictures of its unique animals, of its beautiful scenes, and so on. Once we joked, "Mr. Gallagher moved a total

The Sister Chambers

Side gate to
Peking University

Weiming Lake

Peking University library

Aerial view of campus

Biking on campus

The stone bridge at
West Gate

Dorm living

Mr. Tony and students, 1995

Exams

Australia to Beida." Now, I feel myself begin to like Australia, too. Maybe it is because that I have known it bit by bit. But it's sure to have a lot to do with Mr. Gallagher.

Time goes by quickly. It goes to the end of this semester and the course given by Mr. Gallagher is going to conclude. Looking back through the past days when I was with Mr. Gallagher, I feel that I have learned a lot from him, both in my extensive reading English lesson and in life. Through the "Life's Instructions" he gave us to read, I have learned a lot about how to get along with others. And through Mr. Gallagher himself, I learn responsibility to one's work and a positive attitude toward life. "Do not complain in your essay," he once said when talking about compositions, "try to get the solutions and be more positive." Mr. Gallagher is my first foreign English teacher and also the first Australian I know. The memory of him, I think, is pleasant and unforgettable.

Lan Aisong
History
YUNNAN PROVINCE

My First Foreign Teacher's Teaching

One half semester ago, when I heard I had been admitted to Band 5 class, I was filled with joy because I knew I would have a foreign teacher teach me English. Half a semester later, I am both satisfied and a little disappointed, partly due to my expecting far too much.

The chief reason why I feel satisfied is the debating-system introduced by you. The main drawback in Chinese traditional education lies in the lack of activity. All the knowledge we have learned has been hammered into our heads. The debating system has brought vigor to us and given us the chance to learn from each other and express our ideas verbally. Through this I feel my ability of expression has been enhanced. On the average, the result is positive, but the class still lacks enough activity. I have a tip for this. Each group might as well be divided into two sub-groups, namely, one in favor of some opinion, while the other is against it. This method may bring some competition and consequently more activity.

The second reason lies in the compositions assigned by you. The frequency of writing is much higher than before, which does much good to us. In terms of my own experience, I find composition is a good means of testing and improving. By writing, you can find defects in your English skills and become familiar and fluent with what you learn. Having written so many since the semester started, I feel my ability of writing is greatly enhanced. But in my opinion, there still exists a chance for improvement. Though the number of compositions is high, the styles are comparatively monotonous. Many forms practical to us, such as letters, we have not yet used.

The third reason I am satisfied is the English Corner. I am so regretful that I have compulsory courses both on Monday and Wednesday afternoons. I have often heard that speaking with foreigners can greatly improve your English level. Though I haven't gone to English Corner, I think that's a good idea.

As I have said, though I benefit a lot from your new methods, I am still a little disappointed, because you give us chances to express ourselves, but neglect to give us tools for expression. Each time we complete a composition, you only correct some spelling and other such things. These are important to us, but we can only write in certain ways. Without a model or comparison, we still don't know how to express ourselves any better. I think, you might give us some advice: for example, write some of my sentences in a more correct English way. In addition, interesting as those Australian Government materials are, they haven't had the expected effect, because of their difficult English. In my opinion, some selected Australian students' compositions would be better.

Such views are all based on my personal experience and thoughts, many of which are subjective. It is true that it is difficult to please everyone, and I appreciate that teaching is more difficult than studying. I hope my advice can help you teach better.

Zhu Jinmin
Computer Science
HUBEI PROVINCE

EACH TIME CLASSES MET I tried to set aside ten minutes for small group work in oral English. The Thursday morning class loved those sessions. After ten minutes, a student appointed by each group would dutifully report to the class. During one lesson we got to the last group and they refused to report. They said there was nothing to add to the previous groups' comments, so they had nothing to say. I was happy to see this display of independence. By showing they weren't prepared to just go through the motions I knew I was sparking up some genuine interest. I could see it in their faces.

So, I ask somewhat rhetorically at the end of this chapter, which system of education is best: the Chinese approach, or the one which molded me? Take one Chinese view of scholarly success in English, for example, where a favorite field of study is linguistics, owing to its being specialized and beyond political suspicion. A former head of the English Department at Beida told me academic success comes from sticking to a specialty, minding your own business and keeping your nose clean. To a large extent, that person was right. But does this attitude satisfy the human spirit, or quench it?

In the second half of semesters, when classes knew me better, I gave three-minute talks about my favorite English writers. I'm fond of Samuel Johnson, so I once mentioned James Boswell's well-known biography and suggested they try to read it sometime during their lifetime.

At the beginning of this book I mentioned that, at one time, two of my former students, Ma and Zhang, came to visit me at my apartment. You no doubt remember that they expressed surprise that I wanted to write a book when I obviously knew so little about China. One morning early in third semester, when I was walking in the fresh air during class break, Zhang suddenly appeared.

"Mr. Tony, I can't stop. I'm in a hurry," she said. "Please, what was the name of the biography you mentioned last semester?" And then I thought, "Zhang, how wonderful! You've been listening!"

So I replied. "His name was Samuel Johnson. I'm sure you'll find his works in the library."

CHAPTER 5

Youth and the Pursuit of Happiness

Next time you fall into a fantasy and crave for something beyond your reach, look closely at what you already have: maybe vigorous youth, a deep zest for life, profound thinking, resourcefulness or ingenuity. If you assert that you have none of these things, then at least you have eyes and ears. They give to you the bliss of detecting the world's thrilling beauty: the first cock crow at dawn, the sight of the rising sun glittering on trees and grass, the call of birds at twilight, the roaming clouds, the silver moon. These are all blessings of life, of God. At least you can value them. Then you will be on the way to enhancing the freshness and fullness of your everyday life.

—**Dai Dadi** ♦ *Geography* ♦ SHANDONG PROVINCE

SUCCESS TEACHES LITTLE, failure teaches much. This is especially true when trying to communicate across cultures. I begin this chapter with an embarrassing misunderstanding, and end it with an unexpectedly triumphant one. In the first instance, what I actually said in Chinese was not what I intended to say; in the second what a student heard me say was not the whole message and his misunderstanding led to interesting consequences.

By the middle of the third semester at Beida I had succumbed to flattery from Chinese friends and began to think my basic Chinese was improving. Perhaps it had, but not by very much. At about that time Celia, my Chinese friend at North Guesthouse, agreed to go with me to visit an orphanage for handicapped children. The orphanage was in Tianjin, about 3 hours by car from Beijing. I was about to find out that misusing the native language of a country can lead to considerable loss of face.

We arrived at the orphanage in the afternoon and were initially denied access, despite having obtained agreement with the orphanage director beforehand. We had expected this. The orphanage authorities needed assurance we did not intend to use the visit to take photographs secretly or write slanted stories about mistreatment of children for the foreign media. After we made clear our intentions, which were simply to try to bring some transitory joy to the children and leave them some gifts and sweets, we were given a "guide." We surrendered our cameras and signed the visitors' book.

After playing with babies and toddlers, we met some of the older children who had just returned from school. One of them, a boy of about eight or nine, decided to show me some photographs of his recent visit to a park. In one of the photographs he was astride a pony.

In Mandarin Chinese, the word for horse and the word for mother have a similar sound: ma. The meaning of the language's many homophones is distinguished by four distinct tones. Therefore, to be clearly understood, it is important to emphasize the correct one of four tones. On this occasion I forgot all about this. I pointed at the photograph intending to ask the boy, "Is this your horse?" Instead, I asked him, "Is this your mother?" The astonished boy could not believe his ears. He politely asked me to repeat what I had said. So, in cheerful ignorance I asked a Chinese orphan for the second time whether a horse was his mother. Later, Celia pointed out my mistake and I was mortified. Is it any wonder that from time to time the people of the Middle Kingdom still tend to see us as barbarians?

Meanwhile, during my classes I ploughed on regardless. I continued to tell students that English was about communication; it was all about improving skills to understand and appreciate messages from others and transmit your own. I told them that although their English skills were quite good, only practice and hard work would make them better. I persuaded some of them that perhaps the best way to practice was to write as often as they could on subjects about which they had strong opinions or feelings. So they did write, and on many subjects, including happiness, personal fulfillment, friendship, freedom, women and equality, and aspects of contemporary culture.

What better way to introduce some of the ideals and dreams of the post-Mao generation than with Zha Hongying's paean to youth!

BECAUSE WE ARE YOUNG

I remember when I was a little girl, my elder sister used to sing a beautiful song, which I can hum even now. The words of it impressed me: "Maybe you don't care, maybe you don't believe, but do you know many people envy you, just envy you because you are young." Yes, it's true. For every person, youth is a precious gift and a golden time in their lives.

Because we are young, we are pure and innocent, just like a piece of white paper. We never touch any evil things. People and the world are kind and simple. Life is so wonderful that it seems we are just in paradise.

Because we are young, we don't need to worry about the burdens of life, we won't be annoyed by various, complicated relationships between people. We are surrounded with love rendered by our parents, our friends and our teachers. Life is so merry and easy that every day when we get up in the morning, a smile appears on our faces. "What is waiting for me?" With such curiosity, we start our daily life.

Because we are young, we are strong and healthy. We have vitality and exuberance. Any tough task is considered as a challenge, an opportunity in our eyes. We don't fear difficulties, but just grasp them to develop our potential. We have sufficient energy to enjoy the pleasure of sports, through which we also understand how our body grows.

Because we are young, we have enthusiasm and confidence. Since many things are entirely new to us, we have the strongest desire to know all the world. The more we learn from life, the more surprising we find it is. We can have all kinds of dreams about our future and set high goals for our lives. Maybe they are not so practical, but nobody will criticize us, for they are just the special rights of youth.

Because we are young, we have time to qualify ourselves. During our growth, we will inevitably make some mistakes. I don't think it's a bad thing. On the contrary, we can take advantage of them. Failure can make us more modest and brave, virtues which are essential to our future pursuits. In fact, frustration can teach us more than success does. If we are lucky to recognize the defects we have and correct them promptly, we will not regret it when things get worse.

Because we are young, we are smart. We have better memories and eyesight in our youth, and this is always envied by adults. Learning seems easier for us, as we get more knowledge with less effort. Our speed of reaction is also higher.

I illustrate so many advantages of youth, but only to one purpose. That is: treasure your golden time and do not waste these years in idleness or bad things.

—Zha Hongying
International Politics
JIANGXI PROVINCE

WHAT IS THE KEY TO HAPPINESS? Philosophers, radio-talk show hosts, governments, lovers, parents, you, me—we all have our formula for happiness. For Wu Tian, happiness lies in the realization that we must solve our own problems; yet, at the same time we must continue to enjoy the simple things in life.

WHAT MAKES FOR HAPPINESS?

Two years ago I packed up, caught a train, and confidently left Pa and Ma for the first time in my life. Curiosity about the new life ahead of me filled my heart and made me nearly oblivious of the sadness of departure.

Now, I find the wonderful new life I had expected didn't turn out like that. For a long time, I had been busy coping with the confusion produced by the new situation, almost forgetting about the feeling of happiness. Since Ma and Pa are 3,000 kilometers away from me, I have to seek my own way out of the mess. Now I realize one's psychological problems can only be solved by oneself. It's no use counting on others or complaining that life is full of trouble. In order to be happy, you have to learn to deal with your own feelings. The following is my way:

Competition is something that often gives me a sense of frustration. This doesn't mean I see myself as a failure and lack ability. Sometimes, no matter how hard I try, there's always someone grabbing away what I'm longing for. That's really hard for me, but I can manage to overcome it by "spirit victory." In his well-known novel, *True Story of Ah Q*, Lu Xun satirizes "spirit victory" so sharply and to such a point that it is now considered to be a lamentable characteristic of the Chinese people. But I don't think "spirit victory" should be criticized like that.

Whenever I feel the possibilities of defeat, I say to myself, "That's perhaps not so attractive as it looks; wait and see. I can get a better result than that. At least failure is a greater motivator than success." Then, I feel happy again, and begin to be busily involved in planning my new approach. Failing to get what you want is disappointing enough. Try not to let it take away your happiness too, or you'll have to suffer a double loss.

I like to live alone, but have to share a room with others. It gives me such a big surprise when I find my roommates are all like study-machines. That's to say they can keep on studying from morning to night without rest. That's not my way of life. No matter how many tasks are waiting for me, I tend to set aside some time for my hobbies such as music, dancing and sports. But, afraid of being left behind, I gave up my hobbies and this made me very unhappy. Now I come to know that's really a silly way. I needn't keep up with the race of others. In order to be happy, I should be myself and stick to my own way of life.

It is said that successfully tackling relationship problems is an art. That's true. Happy relationships among people are of great importance.

Some people think they are so sophisticated and mischievously enjoy doing something disgraceful to irritate others. Endurance is a highly respected virtue by the Chinese people, but it's not for me. If someone makes me unhappy, I'll do something to let them respect my existence. Then I'll regain my happiness. However, I never go to the opposite extreme, because only people with a clear conscience can be happy.

My last suggestion is learn to enjoy tiny beauties. Why do children always feel happy? Apart from being care-free, it's because they can appreciate happiness brought by an ice-cream. Then why can't we learn to enjoy the small things in life too? That'll make for happiness.

—Wu Tian
Cities and Environment Department
YUNNAN PROVINCE

In class it was not difficult to notice the author of the next essay, Li Ning. She had an air of dignity and grace. Once, when we were discussing the practice of medicine in China, she told me that her grandfather, a doctor, happened to be on the wrong side in 1949. He was stripped of his possessions by the Communist Government authorities, and of his right to practice medicine, a right never formally returned to him. Despite this, he continued to practice privately, and was still doing so at the age of eighty. The unfairness to her grandfather and his perseverance left a deep impression on Li Ning. She suggests three essential components for achieving self-fulfillment: imagination, self-determination, and having an interest in what you are doing.

MY VIEW ABOUT SELF-FULFILLMENT

The main tragedy of our times is the distortion of the meaning of self-fulfillment. Many people are driven to fulfill this goal or that—widely approved standards set by society, families or friends—rather than choose and fulfill their own objectives. In doing so, they gradually lose the meaning of that which they are striving for.

I have often been puzzled and distressed by our educational system. There is no subject interesting or stimulating enough to stir up a passion for learning, only a wide range of compulsory subjects, practical but dull, used as proof of learning for any student who has passed an examination. No mental or spiritual stimulation. Instead, teachers who have no mutual sympathies and understandings, but by their strenuous efforts, stuff our heads with scraps and details of information. We are deprived of the very thing that education treasures: freedom of self-fulfillment.

For a young person to pursue nothing but wealth, fame, and social status is somewhat abject and ignoble. Idealistic young people always have a tendency towards freedom, rather than a dreary commitment to mean ambitions or love of comfort. Young people of this kind are not social climbers and they have no devotion to material things. Being such young people, we are not using college credentials as a ladder to higher social status. Rather, we regard college campus as a staging ground where we try to put ourselves into perspective, explore our roots, and reflect on what the future may hold.

To be self-fulfilled, we ought to have a genuine interest in what we are doing. Accomplishments of real value to the individual as well as to the society depend chiefly on continuous endeavor springing out of a deep and ardent interest in the tasks of our chosen occupations. If impelled by the enthusiasm of learning, we will get the most from what we learn. Furthermore, great ideas or marvelous inspirations often spring into our conscience, seemingly of their own accord. Thus our work is not merely a job to fulfill, but a pleasure to enjoy. It is this kind of appreciation of our work that leads to the fulfillment of our goals.

Imagination is another tool for self-fulfillment. The modern age attaches so much importance to the authority of established truth that many original minds are scared stiff. But society needs vigorous, creative and challenging minds which are characterized by individuality. The rub is that we should not be so humiliated before already-known and deeply-rooted facts and formulations that we are unable to dig out more unknown things through our efforts. Imagination helps us along, making us aware of the sights, sounds, events and ideas that impinge upon us, keeping us healthy-minded and dissatisfied with the status-quo, stimulating us to develop to our full potential.

And lastly, there is self-determination, which is by far the most momentous of the three factors needed to achieve self-fulfillment. Each of us is a separate person. We cannot live for others, nor should we use others for our self-affirmation. It is always easier for us to become what others desire, but in doing so we relinquish our dreams, abandon our hopes and ignore our needs. However, the ironic fact is that some of us even regard this "other-deciding" position as their own self-fulfillment. What insensitivity! We must yield to no one but our genuine beliefs. We must embrace ourselves as we are and as we have the potential to become before we can embrace life or others. We must affirm ourselves. As Emerson said, "The near explains the far. The drop is nature." We must believe in the power of self-determination.

I hold so many strong views on self-fulfillment that I'm now having a vision of future college: a multitude of young persons, keen, open-hearted, sympathetic and observant, come together and freely mix with each other in a common search for the well-springs of human life and the value of individuality. This, I dare say, is the way towards self-fulfillment.

—Li Ning
International Finance
LIAONING PROVINCE

LIU GE, ONE OF MY CHINESE TUTORS, was a science graduate from Wuhan University, and she was very bright. She told me that on leaving school in 1989 she decided to refuse an offer to study at Beida, as that would have meant wasting one year of her life in a military camp. (After the Tiananmen Square incident, one year of military training was imposed on all new students at Beida. This rule was then lifted in 1993.) Liu loved old China, and when I met her she was doing additional study at Beida in Chinese culture. Liu was self-assured, did not hold me in awe, and she loved talking. So, I found her very likable.

One afternoon, in late spring 1996, I needed some medicine for arthritic pains in my left shoulder. As I needed to ensure that my symptoms were adequately understood, I asked Liu if she would accompany me to the university clinic. The woman doctor was friendly, and after a rather perfunctory examination, she wrote out several prescriptions for Chinese medicines. Then she began talking to Liu in a low voice and they temporarily disappeared into the adjoining corridor. When they returned Liu had an artificial smile on her face. On the way out I asked her what all the whispering was about. Liu told me the doctor wanted her to ask me to give some English tuition to her daughter.

So I said, "Why didn't she ask me?"

Liu replied, "In China you don't do this. You need friends, and through these friends you can ask for introduction to others, and perhaps get something. And then you need to do favors in return." She was talking about *guanxi*, or relationships; perhaps the most pervasive and enduring of China's old traditions.

In China, much more so than I expected, an individual's place in society is manifested through his relationships with others. It is a world where specific obligations to people are more important than concern for principles to which people might subscribe in abstract terms. Of course, this occurs in other cultures, including my own, but perhaps not to the same degree as in China. *Guanxi* underpins almost all business transactions and social linkages. Reciprocal conduct is part of it: favors, gifts, or flowers from a friend, superior or subordinate are likely to mean a return favor will be called upon in future. Whether as simple as a taxi fare or as complex as a multi-million dollar business deal, personal connections can be and are used to reduce the price or to shortcut interminable bureaucratic procedures. The trouble is that, at the same time, *guanxi* fosters cronyism and corruption; it suffocates attempts at establishing a fairer, more just society.

Despite the darker side of *guanxi*, my views about friendship in China remained very positive. Without deep and enduring friendships I would not have come to

China in the first place, and while there, friendships with students, teachers, and Chinese families, kept me going. In April 1995, I visited the Zheng family, my friends since 1974, at their home in Dalian. Their kindness, warmth, and sincerity during the visit left me with a permanent impression. The following story about them illustrates that the roots of not only guanxi, but also those of genuine friendship, lie deep in Chinese tradition.

The latter half of the European Middle Ages roughly corresponded to the Song dynasty of the Middle Kingdom. From this era came one of Chinese literature's most beloved classics, *Shuihu Zhuan (Outlaws of the Marsh)*. For me at least, this book has some affinity with Chaucer's *Canterbury Tales*. It comprises fanciful stories of a kind of Chinese Robin Hood, called Song Jiang, who, with his companions, wandered through parts of what is now Shandong Province fighting injustice. Friendship is a strong theme in *Shuihu*, and a lot of the tales contain poignant partings between friends, particularly friends undertaking a long journey, often described as "a journey of 1,000 *li*" (approximately 500 kilometers). Usually the departing friend was accompanied over the first few *li*, or sometimes for several days. As I was to discover when I stayed with them, the Zheng family knew these legends and what they implied.

Late one afternoon, at the end of my week's stay, most of the family accompanied me to Dalian airport where they said goodbye. When time came for me to check in my luggage and actually depart, Xin Bao asked the security people if he could accompany me further. He was permitted.

I said, "Xin Bao, you are like the friend in the story of the journey of 1,000 *li*."

He replied, "Tony, thank you for remembering that."

At the passport and boarding pass checkpoint he could go no further. With much emotion, I said goodbye and walked through to the departure lounge. About 40 minutes later all Beijing passengers responded to the boarding call. To get to our plane we needed to leave the terminal building and walk some distance across the tarmac. As I was doing this I heard a loud shout: "Tony! Tony!" I looked in the direction of the voice. Behind a barrier fence some 150 meters away, I saw Xin Bao waving and waving. So, I waved back and he kept on waving until I was out of sight. Now I will remember forever that in China a friend accompanies his friend on a journey as far as he can.

Next, Zhou Henghui and Lin Ningye give you two students' views on friendship in China.

FRIENDSHIP IN CHINA

Chinese friendship follows a pattern characteristic of an ancient oriental country.

In China, it is not common, as in America, that two people become friends only after meeting once. What, then, is friendship in China? In our country, the meaning of the word friendship has its general sense and narrow sense. As to the former, it can even refer to friendships between two nations. While as to the latter, it is mainly a one-to-one relationship. Two Chinese, attracted by each other's virtue and character, will build up their friendship gradually. Once they become friends, it is always a lifelong friendship. They fall into step through mutual understanding. During their daily contact, they deepen their friendship as their understanding increases.

In China, two friends always have the same or a similar viewpoint about values, standards, lifestyle, or family happiness. They may even like the same film, the same color, or the same pop-singer.

With the developing of my country, money becomes more and more important, while true friendships become less and less. Many people try their best to pursue money. But I think friendship is better.

Today, few of my friends are obliged to earn money for food. Most people want to enlarge their houses, buy expensive clothes, take part in costly entertainment, or do some other things which cost too much. When they can't afford these, they are in earnest pursuit of money so they can buy more. However, when they have enough money, they'll feel empty. They'll find they've lost many things, especially friendship. If they are in trouble, they must face such difficulties by themselves. Nobody can help them. However, if people paid more attention to friendship, they would find interesting things to do every day and feel happy even though they haven't much money. This is because friends can understand and help each other. People with friends won't be lonely.

For most Chinese, a friend is someone with whom you can share joy and sorrow. A friend is someone you can turn to in time of difficulty. As an old saying goes, "A friend in need is a friend indeed." We Chinese pay great respect to a sincere and helpful friendship.

—**Zhou Henghui**
Geography
HUNAN PROVINCE

PORTRAIT OF A FRIEND

Among the friends of mine, he is a special one, although we haven't talked with each other for about five years. We only keep on communicating by letters, after our last talk at the school graduation ceremony.

Nine years ago we were in the same class in junior middle school and happened to occupy the same desk for two pupils. He always seemed to have a bag full of tricks and jokes. We often laughed ourselves into tears at them. During those secure days friendship gradually came into being. Laughter was our wealth. As he later wrote in a letter, "Three years went by quickly, without our consciousness. The bright laughter between us will remain in my memory forever."

We weren't in the same senior middle school. However, his school was not far from mine. We occasionally met on the way and talked a lot. We found that both of us had much to say and decided to write letters. In my opinion, it's those letters that led our friendship to develop further. We exchanged opinions, shared joy and sorrow, and solved problems. When we came across one another, we didn't stop to talk anymore. We only smiled, nodded and passed by. All we wanted to say was conveyed in the letters. But pleasure could be discerned in our eyes.

Our letters went on transporting our messages even after we went to different universities. He was admitted by the English Department of a university in Sichuan Province. Many people congratulated him for that Department is the best in his university. But before long, he astonished them by transferring to the Chinese Department, which was considered the worst one. In one letter he said to me, "You know, my interest lies in

Chinese literature. I won't swim with the prevailing current unless it's what I want." I was for it. I know him so well. His ideal is to become a writer.

Gone are those days we spent together. But the friendship that started then has been deepened and will continue forever.

—Lin Ningye
Chemistry
SICHUAN PROVINCE

"WE HAVE RICE BUT WE NEED LAWS."

Almost everyone I knew in China had heard this proverb.

Wherever I looked in China there seemed to be either an absence of the rule of law or the rather arbitrary application of it. For me, the fruits of a 600 year struggle for fairness and justice in Britain and then America are embodied in what is known as the rule of law. I take comfort in the solidity and soundness of the rule of law, notwithstanding the O.J. Simpson fiasco and other equally astounding decisions by judges and juries. I take comfort that in Australia the rule of law underpins fairness and justice in relation to administrative procedures, elections of governments, resolution of disputes concerning matters of public/private property, and the protection of community and civil rights.

The current explosion of foreign trade and investment, part of China's economic miracle, requires the support of laws, legally binding agreements, and a legal system. This whole important legal enterprise is developing rapidly, and more and more, graduates from Beida are making their contribution. However, the newspapers and the media contain too many cases of the evils of *ren-zhi*, or rule by individuals, reminiscent of old Chinese dynastic rule. Sadly, it seems many commercial laws continue to be honored more in the breach than in the observance. *Renzhi* needs to give way to *fazhi*, or the rule of law, as applied in modern pluralistic states.

For these reasons I found Li Changren's stirring essay on law and freedom at odds with reality. Perhaps I expected too much. Although the essay was written at Beida, it could well have been written by a starry-eyed freshman at a university in Boston, U.S.A., or Brisbane, Australia. In our youth, are we not all entitled to the purest expressions of our ideals?

FREEDOM AND LAW

"Better to die than not live freely." So said Camille Desmoulins, a prominent political leader during the French Revolution. Then what is the essence of freedom? Freedom means supremacy of human rights everywhere. Rousseau says truly: "There is in freedom, as in innocence and virtue, a satisfaction one can only feel in their enjoyment and a pleasure which can cease only when they have been lost."

The magic weapon which a republic possesses to protect its citizens' freedom is the rule of law. With it the representatives of the people make law according to the people's will. Law is the command of justice and reason that is in conformity with the natural human instincts. The laws have caught up with our conscience. What remains is to give life to what is in the law—to ensure that all are born equal in dignity and freedom. The law must be the code of conduct of any government. It is the law that provides a sense of fair play and of justice which should be operated by the government. The rule of law must be the most basic character of any democratic country in the world. Only through the rule of law can we avoid the abuse of power, guarantee people's rights, and eliminate the danger of dictatorship. It has been said by an ancient Greek philosopher that the best thing of all is not that a man should rule, but the law should rule.

Freedom does not mean that you have the right to do whatever you want. That's a misunderstanding of freedom. If everyone is free to do anything, no one in the world will be actually free. The exercise of the rights of freedom must be under the supervision of the law. So law ensures freedom; and freedom is restricted by law. There is no absolute freedom in existence.

There are several essential human freedoms upon which the civilized world is founded. These are freedoms we and our descendants must cherish for ever: freedom of speech and expression; freedom of religion; freedom from want; freedom from fear; freedom to be one's best. That is no vision of a distant millennium. It is a definite basis for a kind of world attainable in our hearts. Thus, law's support and safeguards must go to those who struggle to gain these freedoms. And that is the unshirking duty of the law and the original intention of making law.

—**Li Changren**
Law
HUNAN PROVINCE

AT ENGLISH CORNER I was often asked whether Australian parents preferred boys. I always turned this into a discussion of why boys were considered more important in China, where women still occupy only about one-third of university places and parents tend to treat sons better than daughters. I was unhappy to see that women's inequality was reinforced by media advertising and by female stereotypes on popular Chinese TV soap operas. These images emphasized that "ideal" women looked young and attractive and were expected to be responsible for domestic matters. To a considerable extent in Australia, women's organizations successfully challenge such stereotypes. But in China, whether at work or in the home, a successful woman was all too often depicted as someone who was passive, compliant, and cosmetically beautiful.

The market economy has improved living standards for women along with men, but it has also led to the return of the male-dominated Chinese society. As an illustration of this, while in Shanghai I raised the subject of women teachers with Jin Hengbo, the principal of a high school with a very distinguished reputation. I asked him whether he looked for affirmative action opportunities for women teachers to join his staff, especially in mathematics. I pointed to evidence in Australia that curriculum change in mathematics and the introduction of female role models was seen to improve girls' interest and achievements. He was unconvinced. Jin just replayed tired old beliefs as to why girls are not as good at math. He said he preferred to employ male teachers. They were better at math and they could work harder as they needed less time off for family responsibilities.

Among women students at Beida I saw no signs that universal knowledge of Chairman Mao's slogan "women hold up half the sky" had advanced feminism. With or without slogans, however, some young women always have an admirable sense of self-worth.

One day over lunch I was asking some of my Australian Studies students about images of women in *Liaozhai Zhiyi* (*Strange Tales From Make-Do Studio*). This is a series of rather light-hearted folk legends about encounters between humankind and spirits or other such celestial creatures. Collecting these legends is sometimes attributed to Pu Songling who lived during the Qing dynasty. One of the young women in this lunch discussion was Wang, a Beijinger and daughter of a senior officer in the People's Liberation Army. Wang was forthright and had an excellent command of English.

Liaozhai often mentions spirits and mysterious animals such as foxes who cunningly enter the human world. Foxes, or vixens, often did so by disguising themselves as young women and beguiling men with their beauty. I jokingly wondered aloud how many of the charming young women I taught could be foxes. Wang responded immediately.

"Those poets only said that about women because they weren't men enough to win women for themselves. And anyway the those ghost stories sometimes refer to men as pigs. That was true then and it's true today."

China needs more women like Wang.

Rather more typical student views about women and equality can be seen in the following two essays by two young women students, Lu and Zhang.

EQUALITY BETWEEN MEN AND WOMEN IN FAMILY LIFE

Since ours has developed into a democratic society from the matriarchal and the patriarchal society, equality between men and women in family life, as well as in the whole society, becomes a matter of course.

Like many other equalities, equality in family life also must be based on economic equality. I'm not saying that the amount of a husband's income should not outdo his wife's. I'm saying that the right to earn money as well as to use it should be the same. Today's women laugh at the idea that they should stay at home just to look after children and husband: can a supporter-supportee relationship be equal? On the other hand, from a husband's point of view, it has been a tradition for most families in China that husbands leave the "financial affairs," so to speak, up to their wives. And it's no surprise that wives account, month by month, for every yuan they use, and if what they said unfortunately fails to be consistent with the actual amount, then they might get into real trouble.

What, then, is equality in family life?

First of all, it involves an equal right in making decisions, equal responsibility in educating children, doing housework, and so on. With very few exceptions, the child's first name is always patronymic. I guess that if fathers could, they would make their children all take after them. In many Chinese families, it is almost inevitably the father who makes big decisions. Another example is that if a father has made up his mind that his son should look for a job instead of going to university, then he probably won't take the mother's and the son's ideas into account. It seems unfair, but it's true.

An even more widely spreading phenomenon is that husbands sometimes unconsciously take it for granted that their wives do most of the housework day after day. In the morning, he sits reading a newspaper, waiting for breakfast, which his wife is preparing; in the evening, he sits watching TV while his wife is setting the table, and if the baby happens to be crying, he won't recognize the difference between it and the sound of the television. I remember my mother once said Sunday was her busiest day of the week and my father seemed puzzled.

And yet rather than these phenomena, equality has more to do with the freedom for either to develop the self. In a way, equality, which underlies these phenomena, amounts to something like family democracy. Both owe to the other the chance to develop higher and higher powers. Both must strive to live with the other's defects as well as advantages. A wife should not deprive a husband of the right to keep in touch with a mother who once disapproved their marriage. Nor should a husband feel ill at ease when his wife goes out for a party with old friends on the weekend.

Generally, equality is one of the elements that make for a happy marriage and, consequently, a happy family. A couple lacking equality is regarded as mismatched and could be (but not necessarily) headed for divorce.

—Lu Ning
Technical Physics
HUBEI PROVINCE

CHINESE WOMEN: TODAY AND YESTERDAY

In the old days of feudalism, women had no rights to vote and opportunities to be educated. Men had complete control of children, complete and sole ownership of property. To most men at that time, women were no more than servants who took care of their daily lives, doing household chores and raising children. Furthermore, the conservative concepts of women's virtues, which demanded women be absolutely obedient to their fathers and husbands, restrained women from developing to their full potential. The only roles they could play were weak wives and patient mothers. In this way, many talented women who had the possibility of becoming poets, musicians or scholars led a mediocre life.

A Chinese woman's life was miserable in those days, especially when she was poor and illiterate. Aunt Xiang Lin was a typical Chinese woman of the old days. She was the heroine in the famous novel *Blessing* which was written by the great writer, Lu Xun. Aunt Xiang Lin became a widow after about six months' marriage. Soon she was sold to a strange man many miles away by her mother-in-law. Several years later, her second husband died of a fatal disease and her lovely son was eaten by a wild wolf. She had to make a living as a servant. But her employer, who was very feudal and cruel, regarded her as an ominous woman and later on drove her away during a cold winter night. She had no choice but to beg. On one New Year's Eve, cold and hungry, she died in the snowfield, leaving us feeling great sympathy for her.

Fortunately for us (today's women), such a miserable fate will no longer occur. Great changes have taken place in Chinese women's lives since 1949. Laws have been established to protect women from being discriminated against. Now women can legally enjoy equal rights and receive equal pay. More and more excellent women have distinguished themselves in many fields such as science, literature, and politics.

Girls are no longer confined within the four walls of their houses. Instead, they are encouraged to go out and do as boys do. Today, we girls are sitting in the same classroom to receive our education. In the future, we can achieve success in public life. Things that could hardly be imagined in the past now come true. Compared with women of the old days, we are more fortunate and respected.

What's the suitable role for modern women then? They were all caged birds in the past, but now, they can choose not to be beautiful ornaments in a male dominated world. They can choose to be professionals, or continue to stay home, as long as the decisions are made by themselves. That is to say, modern women must try to be independent persons in the first place, and independence of spirit is much more difficult to achieve than that of living independently.

Women used to evaluate themselves by a system of values which was controlled by men. The focus of it was women's loyalty to their husbands and devotion to family. Of course all these circumstances were to men's advantage, whereby men could free themselves from tedious housework and have more freedom in sex. Modern women, in order to be independent, must firstly try to find value in themselves, shrugging off old values.

Now, many women have entered into the business world and the professions. Their beauty, gentle nature, and carefulness in thought all contribute to their successes. I don't mean they have surpassed their male colleagues, but at least they are sharing with them. And husbands have marveled at this changing world. Indeed, they have had to learn to do cooking, housekeeping, and washing. In this way, women are beginning to have more time to devote to their work and social life.

However, in some backward regions women are still treated poorly. They can be sold and bought like goods. In some factories women workers are forced to do overtime jobs with low payment. All this shows that there is still a long way to go before women are fully emancipated.

—**Zhang Wei**
Library Science
BEIJING

AT BEIDA, as in other universities in China, senior academics, especially in the humanities and social sciences, needed to keep a watchful eye on correct modes of literary expression. They knew they had to do this for several reasons. From a traditional Chinese or Confucian point of view, unbridled individual expression could lead to widespread moral chaos. Therefore any right-thinking administrator would be alarmed by morally suspect paintings of nude women, or novels depicting premarital love-making. And anyway, political correctness aside, any sensible bureaucrat or academic knew that the best way to avoid personal criticism and possible disgrace was to maintain the status quo.

During the second part of my three years at Beida I was pleased to be asked to help edit and revise English reading and grammar and text books used extensively in universities throughout China. I admired my senior colleague, Yu Aihua, responsible as Chief Editor for this important task. Not only did Yu maintain the highest standards of scholarship in her own work and in her expectations of mine, but also she was sharp-witted. We were always on the lookout for new reading texts. One day Yu asked my opinion on an extract from the well-known book, *Cheaper by the Dozen.* Set in 1920s suburban U.S.A., the book is about the humorous ups and downs in the daily lives of an American family of twelve children. Two of them wrote the book.

The extract Yu pointed to described the arrival at the front door of the Gilbreth house of a Mrs. Mebane, who wished to enlist Mrs. Gilbreth's help in establishing a local branch of the Family Planning Association. Mrs. Mebane had been hoodwinked into this approach by one of Mrs. Gilbreth's friends. The unsuspecting woman's appearance on the front doorstep leads to some uproarious family humor. Yu was concerned that in highlighting positive aspects of having a large family and the gullibility of a woman advocating family planning, the extract could be seen as an indirect criticism of China's one-child policy. We both considered this possibility from many angles and then concluded that humor was the focus, not family planning. So, because China was now opening up, we agreed to include it in one of the revised textbooks, just as we agreed to include some extracts from the Old Testament.

Some months later Yu came to see me looking somewhat chagrined. I asked her what was on her mind. She told me the Bible extracts had been accepted by the political overseers, but the *Cheaper by the Dozen* extract had not. It had implied criticism of the one-child policy after all.

Another teacher, Professor Deng, had a very responsible position at the university. He helped manage the English program at the Graduate School—a job that he performed efficiently and sensibly. Every week the foreign teachers at the Graduate School had a meeting with him to discuss progress. At one such meeting Deng asked us to provide students with more reading materials to extend their reading well beyond the set texts. He said the students had asked for this. He then added, "No materials on religion or politics." I bit my tongue to avoid adding, "Or sex, either."

Despite strong formal adherence to forms of censorship and control within academe and government agencies, there were signs everywhere on the streets that the Chinese Government had lost control of the world of mass culture. Literature, music and the popular press had largely wriggled free: much more was permitted as long as it did not challenge the Party or flagrantly challenge conventional moral expectations. For instance, the postures and expressions of the always beautiful Chinese women adorning the front pages of domestic magazines on every newsstand proclaimed, albeit subliminally, that the consumer society had arrived. In addition, the information revolution was sweeping through China with faxes and electronic mail everywhere and Internet links to the world sprouting on every campus.

To give you a first taste of students' opinions on modern culture, Wang Kunsong now gives his views on the benefits of reading. Then, Qi Xiang gives you her impressions of the novel of the well-known movie, *Love Story*. Her essay is included as testimony to the strong preference among students for what are known as "moving stories"—romantic tales filled with sentiment, pathos, or poignant scenes. Happy endings were preferred, but stories of unrequited love, such as Australian author Colleen McCulloch's *The Thorn Birds*, were very popular and equally admired.

THE BENEFITS OF READING

In my opinion, reading good books is one of the greatest pleasures in life. From good reading, we can derive pleasure, companionship, experience, and most important of all, instruction. In short, all of us can benefit from reading.

Reading increases our contentment when we are cheerful and lessens our troubles when we are sad. Whatever may be our main purpose in reading, our contact with good books should never fail to give us enjoyment and satisfaction.

With a good book in our hands, we'll never be lonely. The characters portrayed in the books, whether taken from real life or purely imaginary, may become our companions and friends. In the pages of the books we can walk with George Washington, Adam Smith, Plato, or even Einstein. When human friends desert us, good books are always ready to give us friendship, sympathy, and encouragement.

Another gift given to us by reading is that we can visit some faraway places. To travel by books, we need no bank accounts, no trains or planes to transport us, no passport for entry to another country. Through books, we can climb mountains or cross the thrilling sands of the desert. In books, we can visit the Great Barrier Reef or Hollywood. Through books, we enjoy the beauties of nature, the treasures of art, and the marvels of engineering.

The whole world will open to us if we have the habit of reading books. I'm sure those who are fond of reading must be the richest people in our times.

—**Wang Kunsong**
Psychology
SHANDONG PROVINCE

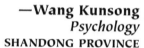 **MY VIEW ON *LOVE STORY***

When I first heard of the story, I thought that *Love Story* was a story about a couple's love. But after reading it, I think it's not that way.

When he was in Harvard, a banker's son, Oliver Barrett IV, falls in love with a Radcliffe girl, who was a baker's daughter. Their marriage angered his father and they encountered financial problems. Jennifer chose to teach in a private school to support Oliver to continue his study in the law school until he graduated and found a good job. But very unfortunately, Jennifer soon died from blood disease.

Jennifer was the kind of girl who had no shortcomings. She was smart, humorous, charming, and in some degree, wise. She gave up the chance to study music in Paris to get married to her Oliver. Even after he had become penniless she tried to support him. Hard work, a poor life, even the threat of death could not defeat her. The deep love from her father taught her that love between father and son was permanent and could never be cut off. So she tried to persuade Oliver to make up with his father and tried to comfort his father when the invitation to his birthday party was refused by his son. At last, after her death, Oliver realized his father's love and accepted it.

Oliver was not a person I liked. He was a good fellow sometimes. He wanted to be the best in both work and sports. His father's threats did not prevent him from marrying Jen. And for the sake of his dying wife he did the very last thing he wanted to do—he borrowed money from his father. But I just cannot understand why, while he gave Jen so much love, he couldn't understand his father.

Many readers don't like Oliver Barrett III, whose son called him old stony. His stony face and emotionless words made people dislike him, especially when he is compared to Jennifer's father, Phil. Moreover, it was he who refused to support Oliver and this made the couple lead a hard life. But is such a person really cold-blooded? He, a busy banker, traveled a long distance to watch an ice-hockey game only because his son played in it. Could such a person really be cold-hearted and yet try to get as much information about his son as possible? No, I can't imagine it.

His love was deep in his heart. Every time he said "How have you been, son?" I was moved. He wanted to take care of his son, but, every time, he was refused by a single word, "Fine." When the son ran away he reached out to him by sending an invitation to his birthday party, but, again, he was refused. For three years he hadn't seen his son, and that made him much older. His face had lost some of its color, and his hair had grown grayer and thinner.

He did want his son to be the best in almost every aspect, but being a father what's wrong with that? He was proud, but his pride did not prevent him from reaching out to his son to try to bring comfort to him after knowing Jennifer was dying. He was "stony," but that didn't prevent him from showing his love to his son, though the son could not understand it.

Fathers are usually strict with their sons. They are frightful sometimes in children's eyes, but that's the way in which fathers love their children. Mothers are beloved. But fathers are seldom praised by writers, poets, or singers. They keep on giving their children a father's love, even without the children's rewards. *Love Story* describes a father, he is not perfect, but a respectable father.

—**Qi Xiang**
Computer Science
HEBEI PROVINCE

DURING MY PERIODIC ESCAPES to the comfort of one of my friend's apartments at the Australian Embassy I would sometimes watch American CNN, or the Murdoch News, Ltd. station, STAR TV. I remember once eagerly settling in to watch an episode from a pulp drama series on STAR TV called *Picket Fences*. The trendy main plots in the episode I watched concerned the question of how young teenage kids resolve whether masturbation is bad (which I admit is an important issue), and whether a priest with a fetish for wearing women's shoes should still lead his flock. I then switched to CNN where I was assailed by meaningless rapid-fire talk from commentators and politicians jostling for media exposure leading up to the U.S. 1996 Presidential election. I knew I could take no more, so I switched the TV off and went to bed. Next day I returned to Beida no longer feeling I had been deprived of the fruits of Western civilization.

Even if they were without English subtitles, I liked to watch good Chinese movies. I went several times with Cao Aoneng, the author of the next essay, to the main theater on campus. (This cozy old theater was bulldozed during 1997 as part of the 1998 centenary preparations.) I preferred the campus theater as I had visited public theaters in several cities where the entertainment was completely flattened by awful toilet smells, smoking, throat-clearing, and spitting on the floor. On campus the toilets were some distance away from the theater, smoking was not permitted, and spitting was frowned upon.

I especially enjoyed the famous director Zhang Yimou's movies and, like tens of thousands, was mesmerized by actress Gong Li in movies like the very claustrophobic and tragic *Raise the Red Lantern,* and the slightly more cheerful *Judou.*

On one occasion at Beida I saw a Chinese blockbuster from the early 1980s, in glorious Technicolor, entitled *Yuanmingyuan is Burning.* It concerned the senseless and barbaric destruction of Qing Emperor Xianfeng's Summer Palace. In 1860 British and German troops callously reduced much of the Summer Palace to rubble and ashes. This was in retribution for alleged insults directed at European envoys to the Emperor during the Second Opium War, but it had much more to do with money and trade. It so happened that the Yuanmingyuan ruins were directly opposite my apartment window at North Guesthouse.

In the theater of over 500 students I was the only foreigner. I watched with some discomfort as British and European soldiers were depicted as monstrous brutes callously murdering innocent Chinese men and raping women. Whenever the brave and loyal Chinese citizens or soldiers managed to humiliate or kill in return, the students would enthusiastically clap and cheer. It was painful and unusual for me as an adult to encounter feelings of being on the wrong side.

As with books, the Chinese students prefer movies with happy endings—particularly those sentimental, but wholesome all-American boy-meets-girl Hollywood love stories. For this reason I screened *Crocodile Dundee* and *Strictly Ballroom* for my Australian Studies class. They were not yet ready for one of my favorite Aussie movies, *Death in Brunswick*, which is full of cultural jokes about immigrants and black humor, or *Priscilla, Queen of the Desert*, with its quirky and rather bittersweet portrayals of homosexual relationships. Nor, and I knew this only too well, were the University authorities. Anyway, huge crowds attended and they enjoyed themselves immensely.

So, here is Cao's story. Cao was a Physics major and very bright, but he disliked his course. Cinema was his great escape.

CHINESE FILM: REALITY OR IMAGINATION?

Films are my favorite sort of entertainment and this year I tried to see at least one film a week. Sometimes when I sit in the cinema I say to myself, "Well, this isn't what life really looks like, but I like it." I mean those unreal films produced in China. And the proportion of this kind is surprisingly large.

The reason is essentially a dilemma. People expect a film which costs them several yuan to be really worth seeing. Otherwise they would rather stay home and watch television. Yet many films just describe the dull life of modern society, though they are artistic. This causes a sharp decrease of film viewers. In fact, the annual total-number of viewers of last year (1994) is one tenth that of 1983. Therefore China's biggest film studios have become short of money. This has rather grave consequences.

A large budget usually means a vulgar production which is not good in art. If a vulgar film is brought out, much money will be collected. But there are some producers who are such "gentlemen" that they don't want to reject art. Art or money? Or more exactly, reality or imagination? This seems a most difficult choice.

A remarkable producer and director has successfully dealt with the problem by keeping a wonderful balance of art and money. He is Zhang Yimou, winner of heaps of awards. He has his characteristic way of shooting films. On the one hand he exhibits all the good things of Chinese traditional art so the films are enjoyable; on the other hand he creates an imaginary society so people like the life described in his films. That is to say, he appeals to the public with art.

Some reviewers point out that Zhang is staying away from reality. They emphasized again and again that real life should be reflected. "Take *Raise the Red Lantern* and *Farewell My Concubine* as examples," they say. "Can you find the same thing happening in your real life?" I partly agree with these critics. Indeed, Zhang's world is somewhat different from ours, but most people like it. He created an ill society and a sad story in *Raise the Red Lantern*, the cinematographic skills of which overwhelm and conquer us. Most people accept this as a great film though there is obviously no real life in it. We are also attracted by the romance in *Farewell My Concubine* and we perhaps would like to live in such a fabricated society. Since Zhang's films are widely accepted, what can we say against them?

And also, Zhang's films have made a great fortune for his studio. This is natural, because nearly everyone in the country has seen at least one of them. Thus the leaders of his studio are willing to let him shoot as he likes. What a creative cycle has come into being!

If China hopes to see rapid development in films, she must strongly support this type of production. As to an average movie fan like me, I can only await more and more excellent productions to be brought out, because I know I will find an unreal but romantic world in them.

—Cao Aoneng
Physics
JIANGSU PROVINCE

ONE EVENING during my last semester at Beida I was walking from my bicycle to my Australian Studies lecture at the Audio-visual building when I bumped into Cao. He was carrying a video camera and looked very cheerful. We were pleased to see one another and I asked him what he was up to. Cao told me he had a part-time job with Peking University's television studio interviewing prominent academic and researchers on campus. I asked him if he was going to get a job related to his major, Physics, when he graduated in July 1997. Cao said he would if there was nothing else. Then he beamed and said, "But this is what I really love!" I was glad to know that today in China bright young graduates like Cao can have the freedom to follow their dreams.

In the next essay, Han Yanzhang gives his views on the influence of western pop stars on teenagers. His views seem sensible enough and his hero Arnold Schwarzenegger does have some admirable qualities. Yet the values Arnold extols are Western: wealth and individual success are yours if you are prepared to compete, work hard and be true to your dreams. Has Han been swallowed by the global mass culture? What of his loyalties to Chinese culture and virtues? Youth is resilient. Surely it can adapt to new influences taking what is good and yet at the same time continue to absorb what is strong and lasting from the old!

ABOUT TEENAGE IDOLS

Idols are modern-day heroes who arouse our wildest admiration and encourage us to succeed. In our eyes, they seem to have everything we dream of. They stand for our dreams and purposes in life to such a great extent that they often play a more predominant part in the shaping of our life than anyone else does. If our future is compared to a blank sheet of paper, they will be the pictures we are most likely to paint on it.

Idols differ from person to person, according to that person's own opinion of what is worthy of his pursuit and the expense of his best times in life. A person's choice of idols usually mirrors the qualities he appreciates as well as the success he is longing for. As far as I am concerned, I choose Arnold Schwarzenegger as my idol for his determination, and in his efforts to change his destiny.

Arnold, a son of an ordinary Austrian family, won almost every important championship in body building and established his fame as the strongest man in the world. After that he became one of the most popular and richest superstars in Hollywood, and earned more than 50 million dollars profit from his investment in real estate. In a relatively short time, he has achieved all that nearly out of nothing. Certainly, he has built his success on his excellent qualities. As a conqueror, he never hesitates to challenge his potential and has an unfailing hunger for success. Whatever he set his mind to, he gives his best and refuses to give in to any obstacles he may be confronted with. In a word, being a loser is not in his character. Considering his success and qualities, I have a good reason to admire him. But most importantly, his positive attitudes towards life stimulate me to exert my potential to greater extremes and remain stronger in the face of any difficulties.

Nowadays, in most parts of the world many teenagers regard popular stars (pop music singers or movie stars) as their idols and show an overwhelming worship for them. They never miss any opportunity to see their idols whenever they appear on television or in films. They collect the latest news about their idols in every possible way. Their idols, so to speak, seem to mean everything to them. Are there really more admirable qualities in those popular stars than in anyone else? Why can they fascinate considerable numbers of teenagers. It's possibly because their attractive appearance and unusual life (at least it appears so) draw the intense attention of teenagers whose skulls are overflowing with romantic fantasies. Since every hero has a natural appeal as a beautiful thing, how can it be otherwise to teenagers.

But a mentally-mature person never has the irrational behavior of a teenager. With their premature mind, teenagers tend to pay more attention to superficial strong points than to those internal qualities which ensure a complete evaluation of one person. But such prematurity does not last very long, and after a few years the growing teenagers are forming more objective attitudes towards those popular stars of their young admiration.

To sum up, idols can influence to a great extent our way of living and can be of much help for us to make the best of our potential. A life without idols seems impossible to an ambitious person who longs to develop his potential to the highest power.

—Han Yanzhang
Political Science
HUBEI PROVINCE

THIS CHAPTER'S END has echoes of its beginning, as it concerns a salutary lesson about how easy it is to be misunderstood across the language barrier, even with the best of intentions.

One of the activities I introduced into the classes in second semester was mini-talks. Everyone had to give a talk, on any topic. At the commencement of each lesson the three speakers of the day would write their topics on the board and then, later in the lesson, they would talk for no longer than two minutes. The talks were a somewhat useful means of improving oral English and boosting self-confidence. Some talks were interesting; some were not. Several students even tried the difficult skill of telling jokes—without much success. Something was missing. I longed for a short speech containing fire, angst, passion. Eventually my longing was rewarded, but not in the way I expected.

Geng Zhu was the biggest student in Monday class, so he was easy to notice. Geng was always attentive, bright, and cooperative. But one day he completely misunderstood what I was saying about the meaning of democracy. We were discussing an extract from anthropologist Margaret Mead on prejudice and the evils of assuming racial superiority. To try to simplify I said:

It's like thinking that just because you are Chinese you are superior, say, to an African—that would be a mistake. Or, it

would be like me thinking that just
because I am Australian, I am superior to
a Chinese—that would be a mistake.

All that Geng translated in his head was that Mr. Tony thought that Australians were racially superior to Chinese.

For several weeks he rankled under this outrageous insult, awaiting his opportunity to put the record straight. Remembering Martin Luther King's heroic speech in the early 1960s condemning racial prejudice in America, Geng entitled his short speech, "I have a Dream."

Geng began by expressing great disappointment that Mr. Tony, a so-called Foreign Expert, could possess such conceit. He suggested politely and indirectly that I was not really as good as I thought I was. He then went on to give a passionate defense of the suffering, intelligence, and integrity of the Chinese people and ended by saying that in the next century the world would see that at last the turn of the Chinese people had come. It was marvelous. I was immensely cheered to think a simple misunderstanding could have led to such a powerful speech. After class I spoke with Geng to ensure he understood the whole of my original message. For the rest of that week, life seemed beautiful.

CHAPTER 6

The Love Thing

It felt like rape.

It wasn't of course. It was my idea. I'd sat on him provocatively bare-chested and said,

"I don't suppose you have any condoms?"

He looked at me with wide eyes, and said,

"Ya serious? Tonight?"

I put on my best pouty, seductive smile, and nodded coercively. He threw back the sheets and slid out from underneath me. I curled up under the covers on his optimistic double mattress as he left the room. Of course I was slightly nervous and unsure—it isn't every night you lose your virginity—but it seemed like the thing to do.

Is this juicy little quotation on sex, on one aspect of "the love thing," from a Beida student? Nothing could be further from the truth. It is the initial part of the winning essay written by a seventeen year-old Australian in "The Young Writers Competition," which was published in The Canberra Times. The quote serves as a clear example of the huge differences in social norms and expectations within and across different cultures. My wife Annette sent the essay to me from Australia late in 1995.

At Beida, initial encounters with "the love thing" were more likely to run like this:

We walked slowly looking at the colorful clouds in the sky. Though we kept silent, there was always playful warmth between us. First love may not be the only love in one's life. From it we get experience, some wisdom and learn how to love. Then we grow up.

—**Ma Lan** ♦ *Political Science* ♦ SHANXI PROVINCE

ONE OF THE FIRST THINGS my Chinese friend Celia and I noticed among undergraduates at Beida was lots of couples and lots of hand-holding. We both saw this as a hopeful sign. What had happened? Among the post-Mao generation was the iron fist of the proletariat transformed into a lover's handclasp? We wondered what went on in private between these couples, what went on after dark: once passions were aroused did they just go on kissing? Did they have orgasms? Did they have sex? I doubted any of the students would tell. Why should they? I told my parents next to nothing when, at their age at The University of Western Australia, I was plunged into the same heady mixture of excitement, confusion, and guilt about girls, sex, and love.

Late in 1995 I noticed a public statement on sex by the China Sexology Center. The Center stated that, according to a survey, 70 percent of college students believed pre-marital sexual contact was normal. At first glance it looked insightful, a helpful clue in understanding how young Chinese got to know about adult love. But what did the words really mean? What questions were asked and in what circumstances? Who answered the survey? The public statement provided no more clues. It is difficult to locate definitive research findings on sexual practices and attitudes in China. It is likely to be sometime before the Chinese counterparts of Masters and Johnson or Shere Hite provide credible evidence. So I knew I was not about to lift the lid on undergraduates' sex lives. However, I did discover something. It was surprising and different from what I expected—I discovered wonderful attitudes toward love.

In China (at least in large cities) it's difficult to establish personal space because there is no physical space. In a practical sense therefore, there is probably not the same opportunity for sexual exploration indoors. The idea of every individual having her or his own living space doesn't really exist. Living space in places like Beijing and Shanghai averages about 3.5 square meters (4.2 square yards) per person. For this obvious reason, and for other more abstract reasons embedded in Confucian beliefs, the Chinese have a different approach to the individual and the collective. Was it fair to assume these attitudes influenced perceptions of love and sex?

At the end of my first year at Beida, Wu Mei, a young woman student with a steady boyfriend, appeared at my apartment door. She wanted to ask a favor. She said, her face full of sorrow, that she wanted to "talk to her boyfriend in private." There was no place indoors for her to do this as he lived out of Beijing and young men were not allowed into the girls' dormitory block. As two of my American foreign expert friends, Rob and Shirley, had already gone on summer holiday and I had their key, I agreed to let Wu Mei use their apartment, commencing 8:45 A.M. the next morning. I knew it was not possible to be completely certain Wu Mei just wanted to talk to her boyfriend. Nor did I feel it was my particular concern. Anyway, they chose the wrong time to do much else as the room attendants made their usual cleaning rounds at 9:15 A.M.

If undergraduates at Beida are any guide, traditional ethics regarding sex are firmly entrenched. Parents keep a strict eye on their daughters. Perhaps this is for the most practical reasons: they are taking a long term view of their daughters' path to happiness. Women in China can have only one child—except for minority peoples, and rural people in some circumstances. (It might sound harsh but what other choice does China have in the light of overpopulation?) Perhaps parents and daughters remember the well-known Chinese proverb: "A single slip may cause lasting sorrow." Heavy social penalties are paid for accidents, such as false-start pregnancies. The best way to avoid social stigma is to avoid sex.

But why dwell too long in this book on such heavy ideas about love and sex? Surely these are not the thoughts on the love thing at the forefront of the minds of youth, in China or anywhere else! Next, You and Zhou tell us about experiences with love on campus, one a sweet experience, and the other a little sad.

IS LOVE ON CAMPUS OKAY?

By Weiming Lake, or "No-Name Lake," on the lawn in front of the library, under the peach trees in blossom, in nearly every beautiful corner of Peking University, you can invariably find couples of lovers. This is also a common scene in other college campuses. Is love on campus okay?

Some people pay more attention to the instability of love on campus, arguing that student lovers are most likely to separate when confronted with graduation. This may be true, but I don't conceive of it as a persuasive argument against love on campus. There are many couples around me, and most of them are hopeful.

Love need not be limited to classmates. Sometimes you must just try to get to know someone. Youths in China, especially girls, are more conservative than those in the West. Such an attitude gets in the way of getting to know someone at two stages: the touching stage and the further understanding stage. A boy may gaze at a girl time after time at a distance not daring to come up and speak to her for fear of possible cold treatment, let alone hoping to create a chance to touch her. After they are on speaking terms he may hesitate to expose his feelings, thus making the bridge over the gap between two hearts impossible.

I'd like to point out one thing in particular, which is it is not indecent at all for girls to be positive in the love thing. It is pitiful yet brutally true that if we compare girls to flowers, some wither before they have bloomed instead of becoming blossoms of extreme beauty by being courageous in their pursuit of happiness.

—**You Yanhua**
Probability and Statistics
BEIJING

SOMETIMES CAMPUS LOVE FAILS

When I was in senior school, I put my heart into study without thinking of anything else. I had little time to play and to watch TV and I didn't think about love. I was just a bookworm at that time. There were a few lovers in my class, but they were often considered as heretical.

On the first day I got to Peking University, I was surprised to find that it was very different from my senior school. I saw many lovers on campus. It was usual to see a young man with his girlfriend walking around Weiming Lake at night. I saw very few handsome boys and pretty girls walking alone on the road. I was puzzled by the change for a long time. I didn't understand why the difference was so obvious. Is love on campus okay? I didn't find an answer until a year later.

Before I came to Peking University I believed college life was very exciting. I thought I could do what I liked to do. I thought, "I could have more freedom to play without worrying about study any more. "I always regarded college as heaven.

But after I got to college, I found it was a misunderstanding. College life wasn't as interesting as I thought. Soon I was tired of it. I felt lonely. I found that I had no close friend in the university. I couldn't find anyone to share my pleasure and my sorrow. The only thing I could do was to write to my old friends in my home town. But it didn't help me very much because the distance was too far.

I began to long for a girlfriend very much. And I thought the love on campus was quite a natural thing and we didn't have to make a fuss. Soon I had a girlfriend. I went to study with her, had dinner with her. Wherever I went, she was with me. I could tell her what I thought and what I wanted to do, so could she. I just thought, I love her and she loved me without thinking anything else. I didn't feel lonely any more and I was proud of it.

But it affected my study, After having a girlfriend, I spent less time studying. We went to the cinema, went dancing instead of studying in the classroom. The average grade of my courses dropped from 85 to 70. I couldn't pass exams as easily as before. Sometimes I didn't know whether I could pass the final exam.

I came to worry about it. The other problem was that I spent my money too quickly. It took me a lot of money to go traveling with her and buy presents for her. I often found that I hadn't enough money to buy books at the end of the month. My family isn't very rich and I didn't want to ask for more. I began to borrow money from my roommates. By and by, I found that I was too young to bear the burden. So I left my girlfriend, though I was very sad.

Now I consider the issue more carefully. Is love on campus okay? I didn't want to give the answer promptly. I think it is different for different people. If one can deal with affection, study and other things very well, it may be okay. But those who can't must be cautious about falling in love with others.

—Zhou Jiefeng
Geophysics
SHANDONG PROVINCE

Zhou Jiefeng's story of disappointment in love triggers the memory of a Chinese proverb, about the need for men to exercise discretion, to avoid circumstances which could give rise to suspicion or misconstruction:

A gentleman always seeks to provide against possible troubles

And never renders himself under suspicion

He will not fasten his shoes in a melon patch

Or adjust his hat under a plum tree.

Perhaps this knowledge leads to caution among young Chinese men when involved with the love thing?

One of my students, a Mathematics major who preferred to be called by his English name, Mike, was quite handsome. Mike never sat still in class. He didn't seem to concentrate either, and I never knew whether he was listening or not. One time, as he had not completed his essay on The Love Thing, I asked him when I could expect it. He said:

"Mr. Tony, I have nothing to write. I don't know about it. I have no girlfriend."

I persuaded him to write, to imagine how love

might feel. So he politely agreed and next week handed in a very mediocre essay.

A few months later, when it was the end of spring, just by chance I saw Mike by Weiming Lake. He was with a young woman, deep in conversation. Then, one evening not long afterwards, he came to English Corner for the first and only time. He had a purpose for this; he wanted to show me something.

"Mr. Tony, my girlfriend is outside. Can she come to English Corner?"

So the two of them sat there saying very little. Mike, however, was full of smiles; he had began to experience the love thing.

Through English Corner, too, I discovered there are some evenings which are more popular than others for budding lovers. One Sunday evening in the spring of 1996, I had about fourteen young men in my apartment. In the absence of young women it was "guy talk" about politics, drugs, and how to measure success. At the end I said, "Where are all the young women tonight?" The first answer I got was that they were "busy," so I pushed further. So the young men said they were all "bachelors." They had come to see me because all the girls were with boyfriends or dancing. So much for the attractions of English Corner!

Now it's Zheng Wei's and Yang Jiang's turn to tell you what they think young love is about.

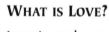

WHAT IS LOVE?

Love is such a magical little thing which you can't see, or hear, or touch but just rely on feeling, only feeling.

You are ready but you don't know how and where it will happen. Love is out of control of anyone. In Greek mythology the god of love is a naughty little boy who is kindhearted but likes playing tricks. You can't love when it is not ready to happen or get it by force when no love exists. What you can do is wait until one day you suddenly find love is dumped in your lap. I still remember always sighing that my roommates were all beautiful but lonely. Why hadn't they boyfriends yet? But you see, worrying is unnecessary and useless. In April, love comes with the sights and sounds of spring.

—**Zheng Wei**
Geophysics
YUNNAN PROVINCE

LET MY LONG HAIR FLY

It's a really fine day today. The sun shines brightly. The wind is blowing softly. I sit by the window, combing my long hair. All of a sudden it seems as if someone were saying to me happily, "Let your long hair fly!" Who? Who told me these words a long time ago?

When I met him, I had very long hair. One day, he told me frankly, "You are not a beautiful girl and you change very fast. Sometimes you have a strong will, while at other times you are easily hurt. But if you let your long hair fall down it looks like—like a black waterfall! Then you are pretty and tender." I was shocked, noticing my hair had fallen down, but I didn't know when this had happened. He wasn't a talkative boy. Yet he would ask me like a child, "Will you keep your long hair for me? Forever?" I smiled then, without answering his question.

My hair is still very long. Maybe it is longer than before. But he left me. We are far away from each other. It is time that changed both of us. Combing my hair, I can hear our voices clearly coming back to me. I asked him, "Perhaps the long hair is beautiful at the age of seventeen or twenty-seven, but it will not be so beautiful when I'm old." Without hesitation, he said, "In my heart, you are a girl of seventeen forever." Now I am nineteen. My hair is still long. For whom do I keep my hair?

Do I keep it for all those sweet memories? For lost love? I don't know. Looking at a book on my desk, I saw this verse, "The thoughts of youth are long, long thoughts." Are they long like my hair? Perhaps I keep it for it's a symbol of youth which passes so quickly.

Slowly I let my hair fall down. Slowly I began to whirl in front of the mirror. My hair is flying, flying again. Out of the window, the sun is shining brightly. The wind is blowing softly.

—**Yang Jiang**
Computer Science
HUNAN PROVINCE

PERHAPS APPARENT DIFFERENCES towards love and sex between my Beida students and young Australians of the same age, including my son and daughter, were due to the comparative absence of sensory sexual material. Or, it could possibly be asserted that this perceived lack of interest in sex was due to a poorer diet, to living in a society closer to survival conditions. I could not agree with such an opinion as many Australians and people everywhere struggle to survive, yet interest in sex seems undiminished. Anyway, such views smacked of cultural arrogance. There must be other explanations.

The Chinese censors remove sexually explicit scenes from movies or TV shows. Such scenes are known as *huangsi*, or yellow, scenes: no yellow scenes for the sons and daughters of the Yellow Emperor. There is also considerably less in the way of titillation available through public advertising or magazines—although a lively underground market exists, to which the students have access. Does this relative absence quench interest?

One evening my Australian Studies lecture topic was "Harvest of Endurance: The Chinese in Australia," and I thought there would be no spare seats. So, I was surprised when, instead of the usual 120 students there were only about 80. Perhaps, I thought, students were cramming for mid-term exams. I asked students in the front row where everyone was and I was told they were "busy" so I pressed for a better answer. It turned out that my lecture coincided with a screening of Jane Campion's award-winning movie, *The Piano*. So I asked a third time, "Why the big interest?" and was told, "It's the uncut version." Then I remembered the tasteful love scene in *The Piano*: lots of nudity, sensitively handled. The students had chosen well.

One of my tutors in Chinese, Liu Ge, the graduate student from Wuhan University, claimed some of her girlfriends do choose to have sex and that the peer group does not pressure them one way or other about this (university authorities appeared a little less restrictive in their views on graduate student behavior). Liu claimed she was not ready, so she did not have sex, but did not feel she was missing out.

In China contraceptives are more or less readily available in shops and clinics. However, clearly and positively expressed safe sex guidelines don't seem to have the same wide distribution as in Australia. As well, although AIDS prevention leaflets were distributed on campus commencing in 1995, more comprehensive written brochures on sexually transmittable diseases did not seem to be available. Of course, my apparent wisdom in these delicate matters is only hearsay and may be nothing but ignorance: my knowledge of Chinese being too poor to discover the truth first-hand.

So, after the first wonderful stirrings of passion, or the "heated love spell," as Ma Haobo puts it in the second of the essays you are about to read, how do students think they can get their love to last? Perhaps some of the suggestions you read below may be worth remembering.

HOW TO GET LOVE TO LAST

Should love last? Different people have different attitudes. Some people think that love can never last and hold a firm principle that marriage means the end of love. Perhaps I, a boy who has never had a date with a girl, can make two suggestions.

First, don't hurry to marry. At first you must have a clear picture of yourself so that you can decide what kind of girl (or boy) suits you best.

Second, never forget to pay your wife or your girlfriend a compliment on an appropriate occasion. It's very common for a wife to ask you what you think about her new dress, while turning in front of the mirror. What will you reply if you don't appreciate her dress at all? To tell her the case—or deceive her just for her joy? I prefer the latter. You may respond with "Perfect!" or "Nothing is more beautiful!" Usually your wife will say you are lying, but deep in her heart she enjoys your comment very much or probably takes your lie for granted. Flowery phrases just work! On the other hand if you respond with, "Oh! It's terrible! What an ugly, shabby dress!" Then you have unconsciously placed a bomb between you and your wife which will explode sooner or later.

—**Wen Xuerong**
Chinese Language and Literature
FUJIAN PROVINCE

AFTER THE HEATED LOVE SPELL

When a boy is in his teens he begins to feel inclined to get in touch with girls, unless he is abnormal. Chances are that he will be attracted by some girl's beauty or grace and he will try all means to procure her attention. He just wants to speak and play with her and share his happiness and frustration with her. On the other hand, the girl may appreciate the boy's handsomeness or virility.

They fall in love with each other immediately. They swear to love each other forever and enjoy the sweet endearments very much. But as soon as the frenetic spell of love is over they calm down and find themselves in a mire of deciding whether the love should be eternal and how to make love last. They just don't know how to deal with love calmly and providently.

Loving somebody means accepting all of him/her including his/her defects. You can try to help your sweetheart to overcome the flaws gradually but you can't abandon him/her because no one in the world is perfect. When you are in the heated love spell with your honey you just can't find any defect. Your loved one is so perfect in your eyes that you feel you will love one another forever. But little by little you find more and more flaws accompanying your honey. You feel a little sad, even sometimes you find him/her tiresome. It's a crisis. If you can understand your honey more you will deepen the love between you, or you'll lose your honey forever.

—Ma Haobo
Biochemistry
LIAONING PROVINCE

SOMETIMES, WHEN HURT by feelings or experiences of adult love, students came to talk. I had several such talks with Lu Yunping. Lu's boyfriend also lived out of Beijing. As I knew her reasonably well, on her third visit I decided to ask her some general questions about love and sex.

After showing me photos of her boyfriend, Lu said that parents in China told their children very little about sex. In fact sex talk was forbidden in childhood. She said Chinese girls were pure and sex was considered a crime. Lu was a city girl. Students from villages or the countryside may have different experiences.

Lu then went on to say that sex wasn't as important, as central to the Chinese way of life, as in the West and that developments in a relationship leading up the marriage weren't focused so much on an interest in sex but on compatibility or harmony. When I asked her whether people of her own age or married people sometimes had lovers her reply was that it happened, that it was not unusual, but it was to be kept a secret, especially from your closest friends. Well, that at least was like the West, I thought. Here is Lu's story about the difficulties of love.

LOVE HURTS

Sir:
Yesterday evening the girls in our dormitory talked about love. And my heart was somewhat stirred. Maybe you can say that it was out of balance.

They said love is just like a dream. Yes, it is just like a dream. When we were in high school preparing for the examinations to go to universities, love was so far away for us. But now when we wake up, we are surrounded by many couples of lovers in the gardens of Peking University. So we know we have grown up. We have to think new thoughts about love.

My friends said we are grown up. Because we are not children any more we are more realistic than before. Every girl has her dream of love. But today we can't say what we want are only dreams. We have to settle our dreams in realistic life as much as possible.

Sir, you know my story. I fell in love with my teacher at military school when I was nineteen years old. In that year I had just left high school and almost knew nothing about realistic life. At the age of nineteen what I had was only craving for beauty. Everyone said to me it was just a mistake of youth and you can correct it now. Everyone said to me that you must look at this problem rationally as soon as possible. Everyone said love belongs to realistic life, and you can't say what I want is only love without consequences. (I know that.) And they said such a kind of love is untrue.

So I said maybe we can challenge. That means we can try our best to change the situation. After some years of struggling maybe we can find a city and settle down. And everyone said to me your plan is so difficult to achieve we can say its impossible. Then why not conclude it? My friends said life is limited and you and he are still young. To continue this love is just a waste of time. The longer you wait the more you will have to pay.

Sir, I knew the theory. I am clear-headed enough to enumerate such reasons myself and so is he. To be honest, we talked about breaking up many times. But we can't. We would rather pray for life to give us a little hope and we can try to challenge. We don't know the result. We pray it will be good. Maybe both of us are wrong.

And many times I say to myself that it's just

my fate to meet with him when I was so young. (Maybe I just attribute this as a cruel joke made by fate so that I can evade scolding.)

And many times I feel guilty because I bring trouble to my parents, for they can't help worrying about me. I also feel guilty many times because I bring more pain than happiness to him.

Sir, I have written these words to you because my heart is out of balance.

There is an old Chinese poem which says: "People who understand me say she really worries in her heart: People who don't understand me ask me, "What do you want?"

Sorry to bring my unhappy story to you.

—**Lu Yunping**
History
HUBEI PROVINCE

AT ABOUT THIS TIME, mid 1995, a charming and beautiful 23 year-old student gave me a deeper perspective on the interrelationship between compatibility, marriage and the love thing. What I learned was not quite what I expected.

Feng Xiali, or "Li," a graduate student in Chinese culture at Peking University, happened to meet me because I needed a new Chinese language tutor. As you are about to discover, Li decided she had to pass through the door of marriage in order to take her place in the modern world, and this was painful for her. At first I did not believe that her decision was based just on friendship. I did not believe that passion and romance were more or less absent. To explain, I shall soon take you on a little journey out of Beijing.

Every week for about a year Li and I helped one another understand our different languages and cultures. In the process we became close friends. As the

1996 summer vacation approached and my teaching and editing work began to ease, Li told me she needed to return home to register her forthcoming marriage. So I asked her whether she was excited about getting married. She told me somewhat crossly that her decision had nothing to do with Western views of romantic love. She said that what I needed to realize was that being married meant she would be in a position to accompany her husband-to-be, Wang, a top Ph.D. computer graduate from Tsinghua University, to the U.S.A. Li invited me to visit her home town, Rudong, for about a week, to see how the ordinary rural Chinese live and to join in her wedding feasts. I jumped at the offer as I was tired of living in crowded Beijing. Besides, I was curious to know just how passionate she really was about Wang.

I had met Wang several times. He was a gentle kind of guy. It was obvious to everyone that Wang was head-over-heels in love with Li. Yet she always seemed rather businesslike and lukewarm in response.

Li's hometown was in Jiangsu Province. Jiangsu, "land of fish and rice" and home to about 65 million people, has been at the economic heart of China for more than 700 years. Today, in addition to its agricultural output, prosperous Jiangsu produces chemicals, textiles and many kinds of electronic and other machines, especially around cities like Nanjing, Wuxi and Yangzhou. Li's hometown, however, was a long way from frenetic industrial expansion, and from well-known tourist towns such as Hangzhou. Rudong was on the quieter, northern side of the mighty Yangtze river, not that far from Shanghai.

My express train ride from Beijing to the capital of Jiangsu, Nanjing, was comfortable, although I knew that outside in the driving rain it was very different—a vast green countryside where too much rain had meant crops were badly waterlogged or even ruined. It was due to this serious flooding that at Nanjing my sense of security

suddenly ended. At old Nanjing's overcrowded ferry terminal, Li's younger brother and I waited and waited,
from 6 P.M. until 4 A.M. the following morning, for a
huge and dirty ferry. Ultimately it arrived and took me
(and about three thousand other passengers) on a rather
hazardous ten-hour journey to the old port of Nantong,
down and across the vast, swollen, yellow Yangtze.
Rudong was a further two-hour bus ride from Nantong.
By the time the journey ended I was exhausted.

On arrival, I was greeted by Li and given the com-
forts of a room to myself in her parents' home, which was
in a typical, but new, apartment block. As Li's parents had
many brothers and sisters living in the district, there were
always friends or relatives visiting the apartment. Round
the clock I witnessed and participated in everything leading up to the wedding feasts—laughter, kindness, courtesy, parental weariness and sadness, family stomach
upsets and toothaches. All-in-all, I found it a delight after
Beijing to be in the green countryside breathing clean air,
to actually see clouds in the sky. My host family's apartment block was on the outskirts of Rudong, so I took
many early morning walks into the fertile fields.

As it was late July, it was very hot indeed.
Sometimes, during the heat of the day, just standing was
enough to raise a sweat. So we had long midday siestas
on hard bamboo beds covered with woven reed mats to
absorb perspiration. At night the temperature dropped
very slightly but then the cunning mosquitoes began
their busy work. Despite these discomforts, I really
enjoyed myself. I was immersed in Chinese family life.

As Li's dad retired early due to illness and her
mother had but a primary schoolteacher's income, I
knew my hosts were not well-off. But the family insisted
on meeting my every need. On day two I decided to make
a contribution to household expenses, especially as wedding feasts had to be paid for. I suspected this would

breach Chinese custom and that Li would resist so I secretly put some American dollars in an empty blue porcelain incense burner. This was on a large side table in the main room in front of the image of the household goddess, Guanyin.

Late next day the money was discovered. Li sternly lectured me, insisting I take the money back. She threw it on my bamboo bed saying,

"You should understand Chinese ways by now. Take this money back. You are embarrassing my family."

But this was a once-in-a-lifetime opportunity and I saw the money as a gift. So again I left it with Guanyin.

One day Li and I took a leisurely bike ride in the heat to her uncle's comfortable farmhouse. Three generations lived there as well as a ferocious dog and several caged birds including one who could be coaxed to say "hello" and several other things in Chinese. After a chat and a tour of the tiny farm, which was run by the womenfolk as the men worked in Rudong, I ate a simple family lunch of noodles, finely chopped pork, onion, and chili. I also drank beer and Coke and watched television where I saw Chinese and Aussie Olympic athletes competing at Atlanta! Then we all had a leisurely afternoon siesta.

On the way back to Rudong I decided to ask Li why she was marrying Wang, whether she was passionately in love with him.

"No, I've told you before," she said. "That kind of stuff comes later. I know he cares for me and that is enough."

A day or two later, while on our bicycles in the center of Rudong, Li and I dropped in on her grandparents who lived in an eighty or ninety-year old city house where Li had spent much of her childhood. Like many old homes in Rudong, it comprised four simple rooms with mud floors and electric light, but no plumbing. Her grandparents were happy, healthy, and independent. At the old family home I saw a faded photograph, in the center of which, surrounded by loving family members, sat a beaming, ten year-old Li. I was saddened as I realized that by marrying and going to America Li was likely to permanently sever these warm and deep family connections.

At Li's request, rather late on the very last night of our visit, she, Wang and I again rode our bicycles to the old house. In the moonlight the narrow alleyways looked beautiful. Yet somehow I could tell this was not a reflection of Li's mood. Li was tense. Although she chatted cheerfully to her grandparents who were already in their beds, she knew all the while this might be her last visit. Therefore, it was difficult, poignant. Li's chosen path led to a different kind of future, one from which there was no way back to this kind of past, a past which she loved and to which she owed so much.

The unostentatious wedding feasts were held on the last two nights in one of Rudong's better restaurants. There were no speeches to the bride and groom or other such rituals I normally associated with weddings back home in Australia. The first evening was for family. The second, for friends, was more boisterous; it included local people of all ages, much drinking and, from most of us, terrible karaoke singing. The feasts were warm and included simple tributes by country folk who loved their daughter, a daughter whose senior school and then university education in Nanjing and Beijing had meant she had grown apart from their influence, had grown away from them.

Very early on the morning of our departure, I was taken by surprise as Li's parents were waiting outside my room looking serious. They pressed all my American money back into my hands and Li said,

"You must take this money back."

So, for the third time I placed the money in front of the family god. I knew Li would disapprove and later reprimand me for my bad manners, but it was the least I could do to repay their kindness.

In order to avoid another dangerous river journey, at the end of my eight days in Rudong I chose to return by bus to Nanjing, from whence I could catch the express train to Beijing. Li and Wang decided to accompany me. It was a difficult journey—over eight hours in the heat on crowded roads in an ugly long-distance bus with uncomfortable seats, stiff suspension and the noisiest motor horn imaginable. The closer we got to Nanjing the more conspicuous the factories, the towns, the urban waste.

In the bus I noticed Li was very tired. In fact, she was cocooned in an aura of nostalgia. Like Jiangsu, like her motherland, China, she wanted to make something of herself. She knew she faced a different future—she had little choice. Through her marriage she could perhaps build a better life. Yet, at the same time she mourned for a wonderful past she did not want to abandon. Like China, she yearned for both.

In relating Li's salutary tale about the love thing I have gotten slightly ahead of myself. It was at the end of the 1995 semester, about a year before going to Li's wedding feasts at Rudong, that I had mixed feelings when I sorted through the 160 or so essays students wrote on the love thing. I would not be entirely honest if I did not admit that in giving this topic part of my mind had a prurient interest in probing into their love lives. But, when I read through them, there were no "naughty bits." I can never be certain whether this was because "naughty bits" did not exist or whether students simply refused to open up because they decided, each and every one of them, that it was none of my business.

Instead, what I found was something more exhilarating, something deep and lasting: 160 separate messages on the same theme. The students said that success in the mysterious process of selecting a partner, hopefully for a lifetime, came from proceeding slowly, dispassionately; from getting to know the other person thoroughly, accepting his/her shortcomings, becoming aware of your own. They said that love that lasts was not about passion and extremes. It was about the middle way, about harmony and balance.

Reading these essays gave me pause to reflect on my own approach to the love thing. Have we in the West been more successful in finding ways to make love last? I would be the last to claim that Australians as a people are particularly successful in encouraging the expression of positive, intimate feeling. I would be the first to admit I am not as successful as I want to be in this part of my life.

I wondered about the dehumanizing effects of commercialization of sex in the West: the negative influences of sexual sensory overload—always available to bombard us from billboards, books and magazines of certain kinds, pornographic videos, and phone-sex services. I wondered whether, through this exposure, our abilities to comprehend the differences between the significant and the trivial had became blunted. Had the conversion of sex into an extremely profitable commodity enfeebled our ability to care enough about harmony and balance?

In the next essay Chen Weiheng writes of the love between a man and his sick wife. Chen's thoughts are a fitting way to wind up the love thing. They capture universal views on love's essence: tough yet compassionate, always unselfish, always enduring.

WHAT TRUE LOVE MEANS

Several years ago, like many teenagers, I imagined love as the romantic things—a bunch of flowers, a ten-page letter and the thrilling words, "I love you." Little by little, I came to realize that love should mean much more than that. But what true love meant was still beyond me. It was not until I met an old couple that I got an insight into true love.

Last spring, I fell ill and lived in hospital. An old couple lived in the room next to me. It appeared they were in their fifties. The woman was in a bad condition. It was said she was suffering from two kinds of illnesses that probably would cause death within three or four months. The man was always on the run; fetching medicine, feeding his wife, washing clothes, going shopping to buy some nutriment.

One afternoon, when walking into the washroom, I saw the old man with his back to me. The tap near him was running and the water had already spilled out of the washbasin. But the man seemed in another world and just stood still. I walked near to him and was shocked to see tears streaming down his face. Something stirred in my heart. When with his wife, he always tried to pull himself together and encouraged her with a smile on his face. Perhaps at that moment he could not hold himself in any more. I sensed the deep suffering within him, and also, the deep love for his wife in his heart. So I knew, to love someone never means you can just draw happiness from it. When the one you love is suffering, the love will definitely load you with suffering too. I believe that true love can survive the suffering and thus became stronger.

Several days later, after lunch I went for a walk. When passing by the couples' ward, I saw the door had been left ajar. I glanced inside and a moving scene caught my eyes at once. The woman was asleep on the bed. The man sat near the bed and his arms were resting on the bed. With his head resting on his arms he was also asleep. What moved me most was that they had their hands joined together! I knew by joining hands they could join their hearts together. They could transfer the fear of impending death, they could confront the cruelty of reality. Love brings one strength and courage to struggle with adversity.

Later, I was discharged from the hospital but the love between the old couple had deeply impressed me. From them, I knew life is seldom a smooth highway and love is not always connected with romantic things. True love means sharing not only joy but also hardship. True love is a hand reaching to you when you stumble and fall. True love is a torch ahead of you when you are lost. True love is the source of strength and courage.

—**Chen Weiheng**
Japanese Language
GANSU PROVINCE

LATE WINTER IN BEIJING is dry, blustery and cold. But once spring really arrives and the spring blossoms begin, the mood changes. Life becomes sweeter, more benign. The grasses begin to grow again reminding us that love is perennial too. Then the migratory swifts and swallows appear in their tens of thousands to nest in the overhanging eaves of all the old buildings on campus.

In my second spring at Beida some of my classes were in the evening. To get to class I had to ride my bicycle around Weiming Lake. Some of the evenings were so beautiful I would stop for a few minutes to enjoy the balmy sunset and the puffs of warm breeze. Hundreds of students and other Beida people were out there as well, some perhaps enmeshed in the love thing, and others just enjoying an atmosphere which made words rather trite, rather inadequate.

After these little meditations I would arrive at class where, outside the windows, the swifts on the wing competed with one another for flying insects. Their chattering was almost too loud for the lesson to proceed. But I didn't mind, I was calm. The swifts were migratory, they were free and beautiful. The swifts needed no visas or passports. I had seen them in Australia. They were part of the love thing. They reminded me of home.

CHAPTER 7

China: Yesterday and Today

It seems that our large cities are becoming more violent and full of trouble. Whenever you turn on the radio or tele-vision there are reports about killings, robberies, larcenies and deadly accidents. The public record states that there has been over three hundred people killed under automo-bile tires in Beijing from January to September this year. No one knows when, where, and to whom mishaps will hap-pen in future. So it's really important to take precautions and learn how to keep safe in everyday life.

—**Dong Lan** ♦ *Russian Language* ♦ SHANDONG PROVINCE

FROM TIME TO TIME, and to my personal delight, one of my students, Lin Erxiang, would arrive at my apart-ment to talk about old Chinese legends and poetry. You can taste of this delight later in this chapter when you read Lin's interpretation of part of a classical poem.

Lin was one of the first students I came to know at Beida and one of the most gifted. No compulsory entrance examinations for Lin: she was invited to enter Peking University. Although she wanted to enroll in the Chinese Department and immerse herself in ancient books, her mother told her she must get a good job. So she enrolled in International Economics, the glamour Humanities Department, and became one of that

Department's best students. Lin was tiny, her language exquisite, her adherence to traditional values cast in pure, ancient Chinese bronze. I was enchanted when she spoke. China's rich cultural traditions came alive; there was no embarrassment or artificiality, just dignity ease and grace. And why not? It was hers; she was talking of her own 5,000 year-old legacy.

So, her love for the China of yesterday got me thinking. Others of the post-Mao generation have also inherited the China of yesterday. Will it survive? Do they care for it as much as Lin?

One day we were discussing religion and what was meant by the notion of a "good person." I asked her whether she believed humans had a spiritual dimension. With consummate ease she gave me a typically rich Chinese answer. She said she might need religion of one kind or another sometime: Taoism was good for those who did not succeed in the eyes of the world or who found such success meaningless; Confucianism (because of its upright social codes) was for those who do succeed, as it helped them to remain virtuous and effective in serving the people; and Buddhism was for those who experienced unexpected personal grief, suffering or emptiness.

I found Lin's answer vaguely uncomfortable. It was completely outside world views in which I had been born and bred. It did not fit into the assumptions, the comforting certainties, of either monotheism or the scientific method. In my experience, adults of sound and settled mind that I knew and respected in Australia either took an (albeit fuzzy) religious view of the meaning of life, or abandoned that altogether in favor of what science and reason postulated. Or, like myself, became rather dualistic. But all of us seemed to have found a *raison d'être* which lay comfortably within the paradigms of monotheism and the scientific method. It was as if we were supremely confident no other overarching explanations were possible. Yet here was Lin being entirely comfortable with a completely different approach, an approach that was neither a priori nor a posteriori.

I knew a bit about Confucianism and Buddhism before coming to China, but I had very little comprehension of the Tao. Laozi, who is said to have lived around 600 B.C., is attributed with the brief and enigmatic Taoist scripture from which other Taoist books emerged. These writings advocate non-interference as the way to contentment and fulfillment. That is, minimum government of countries or peoples' lives and moderation of all forms of desire. For Taoists, inner peace comes from abandoning the sham and glitter of materialism, of almost replacing desire with a kind of harmonious integration into the stream of human existence. Here is a description of the Taoist view of goodness by Hao Yanzhong.

GOOD AND EVIL

A person possessing the highest good is like water. Water nurtures thousands of things but does not contend with them, is content to dwell where masses of people hate to stay. Such a person behaves nearly the same as Tao (a kind of religion): in office he is modest and considerate to his inferior; in meditation he is void, quiet and profound; in confrontation he is benevolent and philanthropic; in conversation he is faithful and honest; when governing he is good at equanimity and non-action; on social occasions he is flexible and obedient; in action he abides by fortune and yields to directions. Because he contends with no one, he has no complaints or failures.

In ancient China good people behaved calmly and sedately. They were attentive and desireless. There is an old story in China as follows: Yangtze when traveling during the Song dynasty, stayed at an inn. The owner of the inn had two concubines, one was beautiful and the other was

ugly. The owner valued the ugly, not the beautiful. Yangtze asked for the reasons. He replied,
"The beautiful is arrogant because she thinks
herself beautiful, so I don't think she is beautiful.
The ugly is obedient because she thinks herself
ugly, so I don't think she is ugly." Yangtze said,
"Remember this, my students! Will not a man
with high morality who does not consider himself
wise and virtuous be greeted with respect wherever he goes?"

—Hao Yanzhong
Astronomy
JIANGSU PROVINCE

AFTER THE FIRST YEAR I began to notice traces of Taoism
in activities around campus and in the attitudes of some
of the students. For example Zhong Gang, in the next
essay, talks of leisure as a means of restoring one's inner
balance. In some ways, what she hoped to achieve
through leisure was a state of detachment and tranquillity—a Taoist state of mind.

LEISURE

I'm fond of leisure. I love it for the belief that
through it I can enjoy life fully. For me
leisure is an essence in life. To appreciate
the beauty of world, to discover the subtle meaning of life, to understand the happiness of work,
we have to take our time and make the best of our
leisure.

Maybe someone will say that it's a waste of
time to enjoy leisure. Then I'll counter him with
it's a waste of life to ignore our leisure. The world
is unlimited, while our lives are limited. If all we
do is become absorbed in work forever without
taking a deep breath for rest, without looking up

into the sky, how can we understand that we are tiny children of the great miracle of the universe, how can we keep a feeling of gratitude and interest all life long? Deprived of leisure, most of us will become a working machine. All we will get is trouble day after day. I don't like sayings like "Work, work, and work" or "Study, study, and study." For human beings, is it possible to devote every minute to work? Must we devote everything to work? No! Taking a few minutes' leisure when necessary does not mean laziness and uselessness, instead, it's a restful pause before going further ahead.

In my opinion everyone needs leisure. Depending on some kind of suitable way of spending our leisure, we can appreciate a fresh and light emotion every day. Please pay attention to the word "suitable." It means we should choose some meaningful and positive way to spend our leisure, not spend it aimlessly such as lying down to sleep.

Primarily, leisure should be a vacation for our mind. We are always deep in work—essential but external action; we have no time to reflect, recollect, and renew ourselves. So we create a chance in leisure for this. Leisure should require tranquillity or harmony, with which we can look over the paths we've covered; calm down when we are overjoyed; relax when pressed; rise up when depressed. I think it better to have a talk with friends, to read some "light" books, or to have a happy daydream. Remember: don't dip into an abstruse book or a brain-drain game. Balance and calm is most important for this "vacation."

At the same time, leisure must be a rest for the body. We exhaust our energy in hard work, we use our ability in physical exercise, at last we need a rest and relaxation. Comfort for the body must be emphasized, whatever you do. Drastic sports or indulging in dancing or sleeping continuously are not good ways. I am thinking of some kind of light and easy exercise such as walking in a park, taking care of flowers, doing Taichi or Qigong. These are very good to relax our body as well as our mind.

As a further advantage, leisure can be an adjustment for the future. We can spend leisure thinking within an easy-going mood, learning some philosophers' method; we can put getting and losing aside. We can reflect on our experiences like a person who is disinterested and thus understand ourselves. In tranquillity and calmness, everything can be clear and easy to be organized. So we can master our past careers as well as past experiences. With fitness of our body, we can restore our energy and vigor. Physical adjustment thus becomes the basis for future hard work. After enjoying leisure we will have refreshed ourselves and be in the best condition. Every new work we face will be a fresh challenge, not a burden. In short, we are ready.

So I think to enjoy leisure is a good thing. Therefore I cherish my leisure, cherish it as it gives me less regret and more hope. For me and for most people it is, or it should be, a valuable and unforgettable part of life.

—**Zhong Gang**
Philosophy
JIANGSU PROVINCE

By the mid 1990s in China the once vivid faith of Marxism had become dumb. Fewer and fewer people needed to make the excruciating moral compromises of the Maoist era. The Chinese people began to have time for leisure. So how do they spend their leisure time?

To some extent in Beijing and in the major cities, traditional forms of leisure have begun to be replaced by the culture of consumerism, a trend aided and abetted by profit-making multinational corporations through the mass media. Bureaucrats, lawyers, doctors, and community leaders no longer needed to be committed intellectuals in the traditional sense. In a China which was opening up, such materially successful men and women could turn to new ideas and ways of living, including conspicuous consumption.

Insofar as I could see, however, most Chinese people had little money to spare and leisure was just a time to relax and enjoy life. Such leisure was sought by them, at least those Chinese I knew, with few traces of Calvinistic guilt, with much less concern that, without relentless, unconditional dedication to the work ethic, heaven (or success) would be lost. In the essay which follows, Shan Dandan tells us about leisure for ordinary Chinese folks.

NEW RECREATIONAL PASTIMES AMONG CHINESE

In the last decade great changes have taken place in Chinese life-styles. A great variety of recreational items are now available, and more and more people are spending their spare time going out in search of fun. Newspapers have even devoted column space to let readers know when and where they can spend an enjoyable evening.

In the 1950s, '60s, and early '70s, most Chinese were busy with the demands of work and family. In their free time they usually visited-friends or relations or went to the park or to the movies on rare occasions. Black-and-white television started appearing in ordinary homes in the late 1970s, and after dinner many people would settle in for an evening of TV. There were, however, only two or three channels across China to choose from at the time.

Dancing was the main leisure activity in the 1980s. At middle school and college, students would try only a few tentative steps at ballroom dancing, then known to many Chinese as collective dances. Soon waltzes and tangos became popular on college campuses, giving way in the mid 1980s to disco and tamer forms of rock music, despite disapproval and criticism from older generations. At the same time, many middle-aged and older people indulged in nostalgia and took up waltzing again, a form of dancing very popular in days past, even in China.

Dancing started to lose ground, however, in the 1990s due to an increase in the number of ways that people could spend their spare time. Business is slow now not only in dance halls, but also at the box office. Many major cinemas have replaced their theaters with snack bars and lounges, while new compact disc technology offers movies with far better sound and pictures than most cinemas. Now when a Chinese couple, usually a pair of starry-eyed teenagers, go to the movies, they must pay anywhere from 15 to 30 *yuan*, whereas only a few years ago the price hovered around 50 fen (100 fen per yuan) to one yuan for a single admission.

There are also many private video parlors springing up, showing a variety of Kung Fu films, soppy love stories and gory horror flicks. Since these showings are usually pretty inexpensive, they always attract large audiences. Pop singers from Hong Kong and Taiwan are favorites among young people on the mainland. In the last years waves of new stars have come and gone, with a new face on the charts almost every other day.

Since its first appearance in China in 1986, karaoke has seemed unstoppable. More and more people prefer to hold weddings and birthday parties in karaoke halls, as they think singing the latest pop tune creates a lively and cheerful atmosphere. Karaoke also allows many people to indulge in fantasies about the entertainment world.

Many restaurants now turn into karaoke halls in the evening. All the big hotels in China have a karaoke lounge, and many businesses have purchased a karaoke machine to liven up the lunch hour. Karaoke machines have also won an honored place in many ordinary homes, allowing families to compete to see who can sing the best (or worst).

China had no night life to speak of in the past. Now large cities are no longer desolate and deserted at night, what with all-night movie theaters, bars, night clubs, and neon decorated dance halls. People who have worked hard all day come here to relax and enjoy themselves.

Parties at home, a traditional Western pastime, are now practiced by fashionable Chinese. Cocktail parties and masquerades are popular among the young. Having a party at your home is a sure sign of "being in the swim," but at the same time it is practical in the sense that it is a healthy means of recreation as well as social intercourse. Some people have opened music salons in their homes. In Shanghai, China's largest city, there are about 200,000 compact disk purchasers. Some of these often get together and compare their CD collections.

Older people nowadays are fond of group-related sports. These activities are fun and healthy at the same time. Many young people in China also like to spend time exercising. Some activities, like bowling, golf, and indoor swimming, can get pretty expensive in China, but more and more people have the money to afford them.

Until recently, Chinese did not realize that shopping is great fun. In the past many department stores were small, and often disappointed people with their low stock of shoddy goods. At that time people started shopping just for the sake of shopping. Now all across China there is a wide selection of shopping centers, such as Lufthansa, and Parkson in Beijing. Passing by these stores, many ordinary Chinese cannot help stepping inside simply to have a look at all the goods on offer, despite the fact that they have no intention of buying anything.

—Shan Dandan
Mathematics
BEIJING

AS WITH MY CHINESE FRIENDS elsewhere in China, at Beida students chose old and new ways of enjoying leisure. A few chose Qigong, a somewhat distant philosophical cousin of Taoism. In the early morning air at Beida, one of life's pleasures was to see groups of devotees of Qigong and Taichi combining meditation with graceful rhythmic exercises. Through this discipline they believed they could locate their inner source of strength, or Qi, and then lengthen their life span by radiating a healing psychic influence over themselves and those around them. Ju Yingdi explains this further.

WHAT IS QIGONG?

To almost all foreigners, Qigong is a mysterious name. In addition, you may be surprised to know that it is not understandable to many Chinese. But if you look it up in a Chinese-English dictionary, you'll find that it says Qigong is a system of deep breathing exercises. This is not a complete definition.

To understand what Qigong is, you should know a little of ancient Chinese culture. There are many things relating to Qigong—such as Chinese medicine, Chinese philosophy, Chinese religion. These are really large systems difficult to explain in a small article. Concerning Chinese philosophy, I'll note the theory of "the five elements." It is the base of Chinese medicine and thus also the foundation of Qigong. The theory says that our world is made of five kinds of elements—iron, wood, water, fire, earth. These elements have certain relations—in certain circumstances, they can produce each other and encounter each other. Thus our changing world has its own rules.

Chinese medicine is closely related to Qigong. You may know about acupuncture, which is based on the theory of the five elements and the theory of Qi. Qi is a special kind of energy existing in all living creatures. Everyone has Qi, and it is very important to individuals. It is concentrated in the Qi-lines which are special routes for Qi to flow under the skin. The Qi-lines can't be seen, but can be detected by special modern apparatus. When you are in bad health, your Qi runs in your Qi-lines in an abnormal way. In certain ways, it can be adjusted. Acupuncture is one of the ways and Qigong is another.

Well, let's consider Qigong in practice. It's a series of exercises to gather Qi, to expand the quantity of Qi and to control it. There are two kinds of Qigong—mobile Qigong and stationary Qigong. Mobile Qigong is a series of actions, while stationary Qigong is a set of moral activities. The methods are different, but the effects are alike. Qigong masters can control their Qi and send it out of their bodies. This is called external Qi. The external Qi can be used to cure patients, either directly or from some distance away.

Up to now, the study of Qigong is very elementary, and it is still a task to study Qigong scientifically. So far, it is more a technique than a science.

—Ju Yingdi
Chemistry
HAINAN PROVINCE

OF COURSE, on campus, a multitude of modern alternatives to Qigong was available. Beyond disco dancing and movie-going, perhaps the most popular was table tennis. Wang Dazhe explains why he was so dedicated to this game.

THE GREEN TABLE AND THE LITTLE WHITE BALL

From childhood I've always loved to take part in all kinds of sports. Fortunately enough, at the age of nine I had a chance to enter the Beijing Physical Sports School to learn table tennis under the direction of former national champion, Mrs. Liu Meiying. Since then the green table and the little white ball have become an indispensable part of my life.

Learning table tennis is similar to learning all the other sports. It needs hard striving as well as perseverance. During these years of drill, I've experienced many fairly hard times: the feeling of exhaustion, the depression of being defeated, the despair of lack of progress.

But why do I hold on? Of course, through playing table tennis I can build up my body, keep myself healthy and practice my agility. But these don't suffice by far. For me, table tennis is really not just a physical activity to take part in like jogging or swimming, but a highly competitive activity through which I can test and improve myself, mentally as well as physically.

Being a sportsman, the goal is to win the game. To some extent to win means success and defeats mean failure, no matter how little the difference between you and your opponent. It's cruel, but it's what competition means. So what's needed for you to win? Many times the gap between your opponent's skill and yours is very narrow. At that time, what really counts are alertness, adaptiveness, and most important of all, endurance. When I'm in an advantageous position, I must not give my opponent a chance; when I'm in a disadvantageous position, I must hold out and keep on striving until the game is over. During my game, vanity, cowardice, as well as wavering in my confidence will definitely lead me to hell.

So, as you can see, playing table tennis not only progresses my skill, but also makes me more durable and confident, braver, and more agile. I thank table tennis for the good it has done for me.

—Wang Dazhe
Physics
HEBEI PROVINCE

AS AN AUSSIE, I came from the Southern Hemisphere. I was used to patterns of events which were chronologically opposite to those at Beida: Hot summer days rather than cold winter days at Christmas, an academic year corresponding to the calendar year and winters in mid-year. Canberra winters were sharp but not frozen. Therefore, I thought the Beijing winter would take some adjustment on my part. I was pleasantly surprised. North Guesthouse had central heating, so my apartment was very cozy and I was only to experience the cold when outdoors and cocooned in layers of clothing and a winter coat.

In winter at Beida a popular leisure pursuit was skating. In my first year the winter came early—there was a snowfall at the beginning of November. Later that month there was another heavy fall and Beida's lakes began to freeze (especially the largest, Weiming Lake). Soon the students began testing the soundness of the surface of the ice. Then the first skaters appeared. After that, every Saturday and Sunday afternoon, Weiming Lake became a gigantic skating rink crowded with beginners, families, accomplished skaters, and experts, all enjoying themselves. You can experience this yourself while Ren Xiaoxia describes the pleasures of skating.

SKATING

It's cold winter now with thick snow on the ground, and thick ice on the rivers and lakes. However, it's a white world full of happiness and vigor. People go out for skating!

Skating in cold winter is good for your health. Staying at home will cause many sicknesses, such as coughs and headaches, because of lack of fresh air. However, if you go out skating, it can build up your body against the cold. Take in the fresh air, move all parts of your body, slide on the ice and you'll warm up and feel vigorous. In the long run you'll have a very healthy body and become stronger than ever.

Skating is an interesting and challenging sport. If you are a beginner, it's important to keep yourself balanced on your skates. With patience, courage and constant training, maybe you'll slowly succeed in skating.

Take it from me, skating is such a good sport that it does good to your health, to your patience, to your courage, and to your skills. It's enjoyable and interesting to do in cold winters.

—Ren Xiaoxia
Biochemistry
ZHEJIANG PROVINCE

IF I HAD NOT KNOWN OTHERWISE I would have thought the bicycle was a Chinese invention. Beijing was a city of bicycles—almost everyone had one, including me. Re-selling stolen bikes was a thriving business, so the more nondescript a bike the better—if thieves thought a bike worth taking they were undaunted by locks. My bike, a hand-me-down from a Chinese friend, became functional once I had it repaired. I never lost it as it was not worth a second look. Though I knew the theory, I never fully understood the practical purposes of road rules. When at a busy intersection I just stayed in the center of the stream of bikes. To a phalanx of cyclists, road signs and traffic lights seemed to be regarded as mere recommendations.

Beyond the university's high stone walls and the security guards at the gates lay Beijing's thriving northwestern suburban precinct of Haidian. I needed to remind myself regularly that although it was just one of Beijing's four main districts, its population was far greater than that of almost all of Australia's cities. I often rode my bicycle in Haidian to visit friends, to eat, or to shop.

Almost every kind of produce was available in Haidian, even if the goods were of variable and rather unpredictable quality. I only had to spend a morning shopping locally to prove that the official information on the Chinese economy was correct: China was burgeoning. It was proof of the astonishing claim by promoters of good news that China was on track to quadruple its 1980 Gross National Product in per capita terms by the year 2000.

As another example of good news, according to the *China Daily*, China's Premier, Li Peng, on the occasion of the 46th anniversary of the People's Republic in 1995, stated:

> With the past 17 years of reform, China's economy has grown rapidly and its people's livelihood improved noticeably. China now enjoys stability, ethnic harmony and social progress.

After a lifetime of work in the bureaucracy I had developed a healthy skepticism towards political rhetoric. As in Australia, here in China, ordinary people had wary attitudes towards officials, especially those who prepare the political rhetoric.

China may be a fascinating old civilization but it is rickety as well. The zip in the good news about economic progress seemed at variance with the very slow improvement in the living standards of ordinary Chinese people. Although apparently stable in the mid 1990s, the economy has been effected by so many political changes, upheavals, and rapid changes in policy. It was almost as if some of the well-known American poet Walt Whitman's words had been written with China in mind:

> *Do I contradict myself?*
>
> *Very well then, I contradict myself.*
>
> *I am large. I contain multitudes.*

So I needed to remind myself that although industry and commerce had developed rapidly in the last decade, China was still an undeveloped country, essentially agriculturally based. It was dirty, overcrowded, chaotic, oppressive, poor beyond imagining. Yet I could not help marveling that in the face of difficulties, the crowded Chinese kept feeding themselves, planting vegetables and fruit by hand each year as well as transplanting the world's biggest rice crop.

At the commencement of this chapter Dong Lan described China's large cities as being "full of troubles." One of those troubles was traffic congestion. My own experience in terms of traffic was that in big provincial cities, such as Dalian with a population of about four and a half million, the buses were incredibly battered as were the amazing trams—remnants of the pre-1949 Japanese occupation of North China. But the traffic flow was reasonable. At the end of 1995 I visited Wuhan, the capital of Hubei Province, to speak at a World Bank-sponsored conference on higher education. As Wuhan's population was about eight million, its streets were busy, but they were not impassable. However, the downside of living in huge Beijing with well over twelve million people, or even more crowded Shanghai with more than fourteen million was that main roads and highways were often impossibly congested with bikes, trucks, buses, taxis, and private cars. Shanghai and Beijing's traffic problems are likely to get worse as more and more private cars appear on the roads.

Next, Zhang Jijun gives a student's view of the difficulties caused by poor transportation infrastructure.

CHINA'S TRAFFIC IS TERRIBLE

The Civil Aviation Administration of China (CAAC) is described by foreigners as "Chinese Airlines Always Cancel." It seems that the backward traffic conditions in China are well known all over the world. Trains are always late and overloaded; buses are too crowded for people to squeeze into. Roads are so poorly maintained that you can see potholes here and there. These phenomena are common in China, except for some cities like Shenzhen or Zhuhai. Even in the biggest city, Shanghai, the traffic conditions are so terrible that most people can hardly bear it. So many people and such narrow streets! You couldn't count upon the buses to take you someplace in time, because traffic jams occur every second. People living there all feel frustrated.

A lot of the problem comes down to lack of funds. The construction and maintenance of traffic facilities needs tremendous sums of money, which the Chinese government can scarcely afford. Another main reason is that earlier in time civil authorities didn't put enough stress on traffic planning. Since the Policy of Reform and Opening was put into effect, the whole country sought to make money, but ignored basic facilities, such as traffic and communications. As a result, traffic conditions lag behind other aspects of our fast-developing economy, and partly hinder the further development of the productive forces. A good example is Wenzhou, a prosperous city in the southeast of Zhejiang province: people are rich but the roads are old and shabby. And in some remote areas, in provinces further west, the conditions are really terrible.

However, Chinese traffic has made some headway since 1980. Under the Policy of Opening, people have to improve communications to adapt to changing circumstances, and make it more convenient for overseas investors. Subways and train lines are improving in big cities and remote and mountainous areas are opening to traffic. The whole nation is facing up to the new challenges.

—**Zhang Jijun**
Archaeology
HENAN PROVINCE

ANOTHER PART OF THE DOWNSIDE was urban pollution. So much of the domestic pollution seemed unnecessary and unavoidable. I was dismayed to see plastic bags, non-degradable polystyrene food cartons and disposable bottles littering the streets and the countryside. On a winter journey to Jiangsu and Zhejiang Provinces in 1995, during no part of a four-hour express train ride from Nanjing to Shanghai, and no part of a six-hour slow train ride from Shanghai to Shaoxing, was I free from the sight of garbage being thrown from the trains.

Close to Beida and nestling in the foothills of the nearby hills are several beautiful parks. I visited Fragrant Hills (Xiangshan) Park and the Eight Great Sights Park three or four times with Chinese friends. What was distressing was that, in the absence of sufficient large rubbish bins and public notices, day by day, the beauty of these parks was being destroyed by persistent and indiscriminate disposal of lunch scraps and litter from snacks. China is now beginning to pay a high price to clean up this mess.

In the next essay, Chen Ying suggests that China needs to avoid excessive and wasteful packaging. He is right as a reduction in packaging is one way to reduce garbage. More effective ways, however, are through mandatory use of recyclable and biodegradable packaging materials and instituting effective penalties and incentives, in industry and among consumers, for correct rubbish disposal.

EXCESSIVE PACKAGING WASTES CONSUMERS' MONEY

When we step into a department store, we find that the supply of daily necessities is getting more and more plentiful. Packaging has greatly improved, too. This is something which deserves our praise. But we have to suppress our bravos if we compare the prices of new articles with those of the old ones, or if we think of the wastage of containers and bags, which can be used only once.

China has suffered in the past by not stressing better packaging in its foreign trade. It is necessary to continue to import packaging machines and materials to promote export sales. But although the packaging of products on the domestic market can stand a lot of improvement, we should never blindly emulate the West. The basic aim of packaging is to protect the value of a commodity. But enterprises in some western countries mainly see it as a way to increase the presentation appeal of a commodity, and to generate super profits.

At the same time, because they have surplus packaging materials, it is possible for them to provide more and more packaging. The trend there is "the more packaging, the better." It is said that packaging costs account for more than one-third of the price of medicines and cosmetics in the United States. In some cases, packaging costs make up more than one-half of the price.

It would be inappropriate for Chinese enterprises to ignore the importance of packaging to increase sales, but it would be equally inappropriate to overdo it because Chinese consumers cannot afford high packaging costs.

—**Chen Ying**
Physiology
HEILONGJIANG PROVINCE

UPON MY ARRIVAL IN BEIJING in 1994, I had rather simplistic understandings of China and its people. But experience changed my attitudes. By 1997, through living in China and through whatever enlightenment the students had managed to persuade me to accept, I had abandoned my comforting but useless generalization—that all Chinese were the same. Indeed, I had really come to see they were not at all the same, as Liu Jing so clearly points out in her essay on her parents.

WE ARE NOT ALL THE SAME

China is one of the biggest countries in the world and has numerous mountains and rivers in her vast land. China also has the largest population and during its long history, people in different territories have gradually formed their own dialects, cooking styles, customs and character. We all speak Chinese, but I can't understand 90 percent of Chinese people if they speak in their dialects. In fact, most dialects in China are as different to us than any other foreign languages, except English of course.

Cooking styles differ greatly too, and you can eat some food only in certain parts of China. It's a great pleasure to travel in China and eat distinctive food in different places. Customs do not differ much, especially in big cities. Generally speaking, the inland people pay more attention to tradition.

The most interesting differences lie in character. For example, people from the Northeast are thought to be talkative and humorous. You will never feel dull or lonely traveling with a man from the Northeast. Morality is more appreciated in the north, which has long been the center of politics and culture. So, most people in the north are thought to be upright, honest, kind and generous, while the southerners are thought to be mean and sly by the northerners. On the other hand, the southerners think they are more intelligent and industrious.

As my father is a northerner while my mother is from the south, I can cite some differences between them.

First, my father is really upright, honest and trustworthy. He has positive principles in his life. He never says "Yes" or "Good" unless he means it. My mother hasn't fixed principles: she gets as much benefit as possible, but also tries not to do harm to others at the same time. If it doesn't matter much, she can say "Good" even though she really doesn't think so.

Second, my father likes a stable life and old things. He dislikes any kind of change. He gets up at 6 A.M. and goes to bed at 10 P.M. every day even on New Year's Eve. My mother is different, she never has a time-table and likes changes and new things. Whenever she gets a new recipe, she cooks it for us. Great changes have taken place in recent years in China. My father has been upset by the changes while my mother enjoys them very much. Third, my mother never thinks that there is something that she cannot fix. When something goes wrong in my home, my father is likely to have it repaired by others. But my mother will first investigate carefully herself and think of ways to fix it.

The differences between my parents may describe the differences between the north and the south to a degree. I can't say who is better, they are just different.

Now, I'll talk about another kind of difference. Fifteen years ago, almost all Chinese were the same. Now, the gap between the poor and rich is dramatic. Today, people in most seaside provinces are much richer than people inland. However, the rich have begun to look down upon the poor. While the rich are making money from the poor, they say that the people in the poor territories are lazy and stupid. What an unfair and foolish statement! One's success doesn't depend on oneself only, but many other factors, such as opportunities. How can you blame a boy for being ignorant just because he is too poor to go to school? There are other discriminations among Chinese too, which are all unreasonable.

We are born equal but brought up in different circumstances, endowed with different opportunities. We are not playing fair in fact. So, our differences in wealth, intelligence, status, can't indicate that one is better than another.

However, I like the differences in our cooking, customs, arts, and so on, which bring pleasure and interest among us; I dislike the differences in our wealth and status, which bring discrimination among us. We can't change the differences, but we can change the effects of such differences.

—Liu Jing
Political Science
JILIN PROVINCE

TOWARDS THE END OF MY SECOND YEAR AT BEIDA, I decided to take a three-day train journey with one of my tutors in Chinese, Liu Ge. I wanted to travel to the relatively poor province of Shanxi, which is over the harsh mountains to the immediate west of Beijing. In addition to producing massive amounts of coal, I knew Shanxi was a treasure house of temples and monasteries of ancient China.

I was looking for an answer to a question. Does ancient China really mean anything to the Chinese today, beyond profit from tourism? The students already knew the answer and had been telling me all along. I heard what they said, but was still skeptical; I would only be satisfied if I could see and touch the evidence myself. So Liu Ge bought the hard sleeper tickets and we boarded the train.

One of the places we visited was Taiyuan, capital of Shanxi. This city began its existence over 2,000 years ago, as part of the territory of the Qin dynasty, for which, in neighboring Shaanxi province, Xi'an is famous. Taiyuan can claim to be one of the earliest centers of Chinese civilization. It is now a center of trade and industry, a big city with wide central avenues, extensive gray concrete residential blocks, numerous factories, and sadly, incredibly dirty smokestacks, especially from coal-fired power stations.

Because of its long history, Taiyuan is rich in important sites of old China containing relics of great beauty. Liu and I caught a local minibus to one of them—Jinci Temple. This temple dates back at least 1,000 years and is located at the source of the Jin river on the slopes of Xuanwang Shan, or Hanging Jar Mountain. It was a crazy and rather dangerous ninety minute ride, dodging enormous coal-tracks and then through the lovely countryside replete with ripening corn, wheat, melons, and fruit.

As it was Saturday and the weather was fine, lots of local people were at the spacious park surrounding Jinci Temple enjoying the environment; the gently flowing clear water from the spring, the mountain scenery and the ancient cypresses and silk trees. Many of them paid homage to the water goddess by burning incense in one of the halls near the spring. Close to this hall was an ancient building called Mirror Terrace, used over the ages as an open air theater, a place to reflect life in drama. That morning there was a big crowd there watching traditional performances of dance, tumbling, and drum playing. Among the performers were groups of women and men clad in bright yellows and reds and adorned with ornaments. These performers created magical, elemental rhythms with noisy cymbals and tiny bells.

I sat down under the shade of a tree to listen and enjoy. Not long after I got comfortable a local group, about twenty of them, having finished their performance, squatted down beside me to catch their breath and cool off. They were mainly young women from the countryside: sturdy, tough, excited by their strenuous activity.

As I spoke to them in my simple Chinese about their colorful costumes and how they managed to cope with the heat, I began to see that this was a living place. That their links with ancient China were natural and real. These performers and their audience were re-enacting what had entranced their parents, grandparents and countless previous generations. It was a simple but sufficient answer to my question. The ancient traditions of China were not only in the 900 year-old iron statues of fierce warriors on the nearby grand stone bridge leading to the Jinci Temple, but also within the bloodstreams of the people around me on the grass.

I had much the same good feeling when I visited a park in Kunming, the capital of Yunnan Province, to the far south of China. Cuihu (Green Lake) Park was in the northwest corner of the city. It was a living and attractive place, initially developed from marshland in the middle of the fourteenth century. Then, in the early eighteenth, during the reign of Emperor Kangxi of the Qing dynasty, an elegant pavilion with upturned eaves and yellow tiles was erected, on an island in the center of the lake. The whole area was then connected through causeways, stone bridges and beautiful narrow gardens shaded by bamboo and willows. I went to enjoy this lovely park early one morning and found it humming with traditional Chinese life: men and women practicing martial arts or dancing, elderly men airing their pet birds, older women chattering, children playing, singers and musicians engrossed in folk songs and traditional opera. For all these ordinary people, links with ancient China were natural and real.

* * *

IT WAS NOT LONG AFTER the petite Lin Erxiang first came to talk to me in early 1995 about Chinese culture that I realized it was as if I was blind when it came to understanding Chinese poetry and art. In explaining what I mean it will become clear of course that I was still only beginning to understand Chinese culture. No doubt some of my understandings were just plain wrong because I did not listen carefully enough to my students who had inherited this culture and explained it to me.

Chinese poetry and painting has a long history. Murals existed from the third century B.C. Scroll paintings on paper and silk began some centuries later, and poetry always accompanied the paintings. I knew that the Tang and Song dynasties (700–1200 A.D.) were periods of extraordinary flowering of human ingenuity. The proof of this lies not only in landscape paintings but also in the long series of Chinese firsts in technology. For example, during that time appeared three inventions that later molded European history: printing, the maritime compass, and gunpowder.

At Jinci Temple, Taiyuan, and at the National Art Gallery, Beijing, I admired beautifully painted wooden statues, woodblock prints, and paintings of Tang dynasty noble women and attendants to the Emperor. I could see, too, how traditional landscape painting was clearly influenced by Taoism. The perspective drew the viewer into the picture and the unpainted parts gave the picture depth. The harmonious relationship between man and nature was shown by depicting people as small, as almost disappearing figures in the landscape.

Nevertheless, I knew I was blind to the real beauty of these paintings. Several times I went with Celia to art exhibitions at China's National Gallery. I could appreciate the sensitivity of Xu Beihong, a 20th century Chinese artist who had been strongly influenced by training in art schools in Europe. When at the Xu Beihong exhibition, I remember smiling at the distortion of English in the Public Notice cautioning patrons to refrain from touching his paintings. Instead of something like, "Please do not touch the paintings," the gallery signs said, "Don't stroke the works!" I could appreciate, too, the astonishingly beautiful and delicate paintings of insects and flowers by Qi Baishi; I could even see the beauty in the empty spaces in his paintings. But, unlike Celia, I could see nothing when I looked at the accompanying Chinese calligraphy, or painting seals. This was because I was ignorant of the intimate association between writing and painting, an association as old as the original pictographic character of Chinese script.

This blind spot also made me hamstrung when it came to appreciating classical poetry. Understanding the poet through the words of the translator was one limitation. The other was I could not see the beauty of the author's calligraphy or the richness of the cadences when read aloud in Chinese or the subtlety of meaning in the interrelationships of shape in the written Chinese characters. Lin Erxiang would sigh when she explained this, and she explained it wistfully many times.

So, with these limitations in mind, limitations you may share unless you can read Chinese, let Lin now explain part of a simple, ancient Chinese poem by Cao Pi. This poet lived in the Three Kingdoms period, an era which coincided in Europe with the first persecutions of Christians in the then declining Roman Empire.

 ## A CLASSICAL CHINESE POEM:

"STICK TO YOUR IDEALS"

First, I'll translate part of a well-known Chinese poem into English:

The high mountains have their steep cliffs

And the trees have their branches;

But man doesn't know

Where his worry comes from.

Now I will try to explain it: perhaps this means everything has its origin but I can't find my worry's origin. Although the poem is very simple and the words are plain, you can find much beauty in it.

The poet didn't tell you what the worry is and what you should do. He just described two images, which are well known and popular, but have some figurative meanings within them, and expressed his mysterious feelings. He used these images to help to make up an atmosphere you can feel but you can't describe clearly. The poem is so simple that the poet left much room for you to imagine. You can find many things behind the words.

Naturally we may ask: why don't we know where our worry comes from? Perhaps because it appears so quickly that we haven't any time to pay attention to where it comes from. Perhaps because there are so many things for us to worry about that we can't know clearly where they come from. We can see the poet just expressed a consciousness of worrying about our lives. His feeling was not light; rather the feeling is a little heavy. He really worried about something and couldn't get rid of it. Perhaps he had noticed that if you are alive, you can't avoid worry.

Then what was the poet worrying about? Was there anything too heavy for him to express? Perhaps he was worrying about his country, or his family; something which had happened, or something which hadn't happened yet, but he could sense it. Perhaps he was worrying about something which would concern others too, or something nobody would worry about but him. Perhaps because he was more clear-headed and sensitive than common people, he could foresee something others couldn't sense.

Then, why? I think because real life isn't consistent with our ideals. Just like in a Chinese saying: we are unsatisfied nine times out of ten in our life. In some degree, real life is cold and cruel and full of troubles and worries. But should we give up our ideals because of this? However, I think as long as we still have our enthusiasm and ideals, we won't give up struggling.

So we can see the poet worried deeply just because he lived earnestly. He didn't treat life as a game and just live carelessly. He didn't just live for comfort. He wouldn't avoid life and betray himself. He wouldn't give up ideals in his heart, even when faced with a cold life. He chose a more serious approach to life.

So in some degree, the tone of this poem isn't merely passive. There is even some enthusiasm under the words. The poet sighed only because he was honest. In short, through the sigh, we can sense a feeling of fate, of something unknown, of something within our real lives. The sigh and this kind of feeling make up a kind of light anxiety atmosphere which covers the poem, just like a cloudy day without sun.

And we can also sense some moods which can't be expressed clearly in words. This is what many ancient Chinese poems express: something you can feel by intuition rather than by analyzing it logically. (In this way it's different from Western culture.)

Now let's imagine a deep-autumn morning. The fog hasn't disappeared and the sun hasn't quite risen at Peking University. Weiming Lake, with the distant mountains around it, lies under the fog quietly. The trees' leaves have all fallen and the grass has grown yellow. But we can't see them clearly because of the fog. On this quiet morning, a man is walking on a path around the lake alone while many people are still sleeping. He is walking slowly as if he is thinking over something complex. Suddenly he utters a sigh gently, just like the poet sighed thousands of years ago. And the lake hears the sigh.

—**Lin Erxiang**
Chinese Language and Literature
GUANGDONG PROVINCE

NOW THAT YOU HAVE READ about sticking to ideals, I can tell you what happened to Lin on graduation. Lin wanted to study classical Chinese but had to enroll in International Economics because it was more practical. Well, she did well enough to qualify without examination for graduate school in economics at Beida. But she wanted to enroll in the Beida graduate school in Chinese Literature. This would have caused a deep rift with her mother. So, what was she to do? She, like the poet, Cao Pi, knew real life was not consistent with ideals but, like him too, she did not give up struggling until she found a solution. She applied for scholarships in America both in Economics, and, without mother's knowledge, Chinese Literature. Lin got offers for both.

So, in early August 1997, as I was leaving Beijing to return to Australia, Liu Erxiang, who had taught me so much about the enduring core of Chinese values, was packing her bags to make her way to a distinguished university on America's east coast. There she would begin her life, and a successful and fruitful life, I dare say, as a classical Chinese scholar. Her mother was satisfied that there would be no loss of face if her daughter was in America.

As someone who believes in the power of dreams, someone whose dream of coming to teach in China had been fulfilled, I saw Liu's dream was just beginning. I wished her joy.

* * *

EARLY ONE VERY COLD MORNING after Christmas in 1995, I cycled to the Foreign Affairs Office building on campus to inquire about my salary payment arrangements during winter recess. To my surprise one of the senior staff, Pan Jialuan, was systematically mopping the floor. This was a task I would never have been expected to do in a roughly equivalent position I once had in Canberra. Indeed, if I had attempted to clean the floor of my office regularly, a Union supervisor could have threatened a demarcation dispute. But I should not have been so surprised. It was another reminder that this was China and I was privileged: my salary as a Foreign Expert was probably twice Pan's—but was my work worth twice as much?

During that Christmas week I received many amazing, heavily scented, red Chinese Christmas cards from my students containing unintentionally amusing messages. The humor made their warm greetings even sweeter. But their sincerity was far more important. They wanted me to fully enjoy the significance of my culture's best known ancient festival, celebrating the family and, at the heart of it, the birth of Christ. Many students asked me whether I had ever had a white Christmas, and even I began to look forward to having one. When Christmas did arrive it was indeed white and I had a most enjoyable time at North Guesthouse in the company of five fellow Australians. These experiences helped me realize that although the kinds of Christmas festivities may and do change over time, worthwhile traditions do not fade.

The human spirit will continue to hold on to the best of the old and accommodate the arrival of the new. I had come to see that in China people of the post-Mao generation are well able to value those things of the past which will never fade and, at the same time, draw from the new.

Li Quan now ends these thoughts about China yesterday and today with an essay on Christmas Day and the Spring Festival.

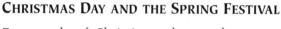

CHRISTMAS DAY AND THE SPRING FESTIVAL

For people of Christian cultures, the most cheerful time in winter is Christmas Day. However, in China the traditional festival that most people look forward to is the Spring Festival.

Christmas Day is celebrated to commemorate the birth of Jesus Christ. During the week before Christmas Day, everyone is busy. People usually go shopping, decorate their houses with holly and send Christmas cards to friends. On Christmas Eve, the family sit around the fireplace, eating tasty food, and watch TV. There is always a Christmas tree decorated with candles and bells standing in the hall. It symbolizes peace and prosperity.

In China, the Spring Festival occurs around late January. It is celebrated to show people's keenness for spring. In the countryside, when winter comes, there is not much farm work. Then people begin to clean up their houses, kill some cattle or pigs and prepare for the festival. Everyone is busy but with smiles on their faces, for it's time for them to enjoy their harvest after a year's hard work.

When the day comes, everyone puts on new, pretty clothes. Every house has a red antithetical couplet and New Year pictures on the door. The mothers are busy cooking, so the children become completely free. They go around full of joy, and without care, making their new clothes dirty. However, nobody will blame them, for it's a time that everybody should be happy. Darkness falls, the family sits down to enjoy their supper of traditional Chinese dumplings, or *jiaozi*. It is also a custom to light fireworks before supper. That moment comes bustling with noise and excitement. Everyone's face is lightened up with pleasure. Even the air is in a joyful mood. The next morning people always get up early to pay a New Year call to their neighbors and relatives.

As an old custom, people used to offer a sacrifice to gods or ancestors for good harvests and for their lives to be safe and sound. Today there are still parts of China where this custom continues.

Compared with the children who have Santa Claus to send them presents, Chinese children have more tangible benefits. Their grandparents give them money, called *yasui qian*. With it they can buy anything they like.

There are many differences between the customs of the East and the West countries. So the forms of their festivals are not alike. But there is still one point that is clearly the same: all over the world people like to celebrate festivals, and the festivals symbolize their hopes for a bright future.

—**Li Quan**
Sociology
HUBEI PROVINCE

CHAPTER 8

China's Future, Our Future

It's Friday, September 1, 2000, and the Olympic Games have begun in Sydney, Australia. For me it's a typical working day. I'm sitting by a table in the clinic reading some files. I am now a professional psychologist and what I read this day are some of the memos of cases I have dealt with, especially case studies in hypertension, a disease which afflicts many old people and now more and more middle-aged people in China.

—**Zhang Tinghua** ♦ *Psychology* ♦ SICHUAN PROVINCE

JULY DAYS AND NIGHTS IN BEIJING: hot, humid and wet. The tourist flow receded to a trickle; students returned home; the pace of life slowed down. Nevertheless I had plenty of energy as at North Guesthouse my room was a haven of coolness—air conditioning being yet another privilege extended to foreign experts. During July, Australia seemed closer. Perhaps this was because at the end of my first year at Beida Annette and my two adult children, Christian and Lucy, arrived, and I was overjoyed to see them. Particularly Annette. At that time, Lucy had almost completed her Civil Engineering degree at the University of New South Wales. What a different environment from Beida! We talked much about these differences. I was glad to see

Christian, too, as he was beginning preparations for a thirteen-month stint as building supervisor at Casey Base, Antarctica. Of course, the students and my Chinese friends were very eager to meet my family, so everyone had a most enjoyable and interesting holiday. After that, I returned home with Annette for a brief break—my home in the lucky country to the far south of Asia.

During semesters, in my Australian Studies lectures, I was surprised at my patriotic fervor. I experienced no cultural cringe and spoke with unabashed frankness about Australia's achievements and deficiencies—past and present. It seemed that from China I saw Australia more clearly, partly as a consequence of having to organize my thoughts in order to teach undergraduates, but mainly because, flowing from a sense of detachment, the essentials stood out. It seemed to me that as we approach the year 2000, resource-rich Australia's future becomes more and more closely linked with China's. After all, by 2010 China, which by then will include Hong Kong and Macao, may well be Australia's biggest trading partner. By then, too, we will probably be a republic with an ever-increasing proportion of our population Asian. Our fondness for many English values is likely to persist as will the robustness of the rule of law underpinning our social and political structures. As for the Australian character, I liked to think our capacity for understatement and our notion of "a fair go" would be undiminished. That is, the conviction that individual achievement goes hand in hand with toleration for differences and, to some degree, sympathy for the underdog.

Over the space of a few years in China, through my students, friends and an inescapable immersion in the pace and flavor of daily life, I had become acquainted with traditional Chinese values, customs and plain philosophies for survival and happiness. On the one hand, the Chinese people that I knew cared little about dogma and related principles. Perhaps it was this pragmatic approach which accounted for the growing success of the Chinese at the end of this century in business at all levels, whether undertaken collectively or individually. On the other hand, once I really got to know some of them, I discovered that the Chinese people were warm and open in friendship and genuine in their respect for the enduring core of traditional Chinese morality and values. I realized that it was through these friendships, rather than through any other source, that my faith in the human spirit had been strengthened. This was because it was through friendship and the trust that it brings that I had been able to listen to words from the heart about what it meant to be Chinese, about the ancient essences of China.

I knew, too, that it took much more than the several years I had been in China to understand at any depth this vast country with its 5,000 year-old history. I remembered that my student Zhang, the daughter of poor villagers in Zhejiang Province, had once told me that unless I was familiar with Chinese language I could not understand China. I knew this. Despite some improvement, I still only recognized Chinese characters at about primary school level. Nevertheless, I had come to see China as a universe in itself, which, for such a long time, had survived, flourished even, without Revelation, the Age of the Enlightenment, or the fruits of the Scientific Method. It was now changing, but it was still a distinctly different universe, full of variety, contrasts and unresolved problems. I saw that, although more crowded than ever, China's citizens were determined to survive and prosper, no matter what.

As a result of these experiences I knew that I was leaving China richer than when I arrived. At a deep philosophical level my comfortable self-sufficiency had been challenged. I knew this was a good thing, a sign of growth. Inasmuch as I had been able to face up to questioning an almost unshakable belief in my own civilization and myself, I had become a tiny bit less self-opinionated. I was somewhat less cocksure. I was not so fixed in my ideas as when I came.

Toward the end of each semester I encouraged the students to tell me what they thought of the future, for China, for themselves. I did this through asking them to write on two topics. The second topic, "My Future, China's Future," is considered later in this chapter. I gave the title "China's Three Greatest Challenges" to the first topic. As had always been my practice, I gave them no personal preferences, no information on those challenges which I thought were the most significant. Instead, we had a brainstorming session where we listed a huge number of possibilities on the blackboard.

These were the main challenges students chose to write about: improving education, controlling and coping with a huge population, stamping out corruption, and halting pollution. A few wrote about two of my preferred (but undeclared) challenges: the benefits and disadvantages of new technologies, and unemployment and under-employment. No one wrote about two others—the importance of constructing quality public utilities and transportation, and maintaining political stability.

Chen Ken now shares his views on China's challenges.

CHINA'S BIGGEST CHALLENGES

Only well-educated people can make a big contribution to their society and make it more civilized. Japan, America, and Russia's rapid developments are attributed in large measure to their great emphasis on education. Yet the present situation of education in China is not at all satisfactory.

Rich as China's resources may be, they are limited. We should use them to the fullest extent. But some factories do not think of this; what they care for is present profits. Thus they waste a lot of resources which never come back to us. At the same time, they pay little attention to pollution and cause dreadful harm to our environment. As we know, nature has its biological balance and if we are against it, nature will have its revenge. Third, I'll mention loss of spirit. With rapid development some people lose their moral values. They pay no attention to things other than money. They don't care for the society they live in or the country they belong to. They only care for themselves.

Thus comes many conflicts and other social problems. Thus much corruption emerges. Thus comes the ruin of social peace. But Chinese development needs the dedication of each and every one of her people. Only when we can recover lost spirit can we make more advances.

—**Chen Ken**
Physics
SHAANXI PROVINCE

CLOSE TO BEIDA there was a very good supermarket where I often shopped on weekends. It was opposite the Pizza Hut on the corner of Haidian Street and Zhongdian (or Computer City) Street. For the worst of reasons it was often difficult to get in the shop door. This was because, energized by the excitement of a quick buck, hawkers of illegal compact discs gathered there.

The next student Chen Xueqin gives his views on the importance of communications technology to China's future. And it is important. In rich countries such as the U.S.A., Canada, and Australia, advanced electronics underpins efficiencies in transport, factory production, supermarkets, commerce, government, research—everywhere. However, of itself such technology has not been a panacea for social and economic ills. Just as in the West, in China these efficiencies will very quickly reduce dependency on human labor, driving millions more of the unskilled and semi-skilled into underemployment and unemployment. As well, high technology is unlikely to close the gap between the "haves" and the "have-nots": even with Internet, robotics and smart cards, in America and Australia the rich and the poor are drifting further apart.

THE ROLE OF INFORMATION IN MODERN SOCIETY

Karl Marx has divided the history of human beings into several stages according to the kinds of tools used by people. According to his standard, now we are moving towards the information society.

In this era, information is essential to mankind. With the development of modern society, we have produced more information than ever before. Without advanced machines to process data, we would find it difficult to keep the society running in good order. Information is playing a decisive role in science, research, industrial production, education, and other fields.

A case in point is the implementation of CAD (Computer Aided Design) in the automobile industry. This technology brings more profits to big companies like General Motors, and makes the work of designing a new car convenient and easy, and saves time.

The information revolution also increases the quality of our life. It gives us access to more knowledge and information. It's easy to reach every achievement in our culture. We possess more information than our ancestors. We are not so confined to limited areas anymore. In a deep sense, we can free ourselves.

In the future, information will become more important. Some foretell that we're going into the post-industrial society from the industrial society and it will be a society of information. Information, instead of machines, will take the dominant role in society. Many countries put a very great emphasis on information technology. Information highways are being built in these countries. China falls behind them economically. How can we catch up with them? We should seize the chance of the information tide and try to develop our information industry.

> **—Chen Xueqin**
> *International Politics*
> **ANHUI PROVINCE**

IN CHINA, WHETHER AT THE HIGHEST or lowest levels, the smell of corruption is never far away.

Wu Suqing, one of my colleagues in the English Department, once told me how she had been tricked into buying poor quality dress material she didn't really want and at inflated prices. One day Suqing was stopped by a forlorn-looking woman outside a shop in downtown Beijing. The woman said she needed help in buying a measure of cloth for her out-of-town sister, who just happened to be the same size as Suqing. Once inside the shop, Suqing was induced to buy other material at "bargain prices." So she did. Only afterwards did it dawn on her that the woman was in league with the shopkeeper. A few days later she happened to pass the shop again. Behold, the same woman was there spinning deceit to another unsuspecting citizen.

The world is full of trickery. Petty sharp practices such as the one just described occur in London, Calcutta, Sydney, New York—in heaps of places. But such rip-offs were less common in the China of the parents and grandparents of the post-Mao generation. When students related stories like this they were disturbed that it was a growing problem. Nevertheless, they kept their real outrage for corrupt government officials.

The idea one could "become an official and get rich," an idea that has its roots in ancient China, always seemed ready to sprout. In the heyday of Maoism, when everyone wore the same uniform, more or less, a few cadre managers tried to get rich by taking it out of the people. Since the beginning of the Reform and Opening *(gaige kaifang)* policy, some government officials try to take it out of the state economy. As just one example of this, a *China Daily* editorial late in 1995 complained about unnecessary use and hoarding of luxury cars by officials. The editorial claimed that, despite a government ban on their use, some luxury cars were still concealed in government agency garages and periodically "walked" to keep them in good working order:

> *As many government officials are mixed up with this,*
> *the task of combating corruption is forever arduous,*
> *and unremitting efforts should be made.*

Corruption, embezzlement, featherbedding, and graft, especially when groups of officials and others were involved through *guanxi,* left students with a feeling of distrust and loathing. Some students seemed to have given up on the spread of corruption and this motivated them to look for opportunities to go abroad.

Wu Xu now expresses his concern about corruption and then talks of how education has been adversely affected by China's policies of opening up.

MY VIEW ON CHINESE REFORM AND OPEN POLICY

In 1978, the year after the end of the infamous Cultural Revolutionary Campaign, the Chinese economy had reached the edge of the precipice. But just in this year, an important people's Congress was held—the Third Congress of the Eleventh Central Committee, from which the reform policy originated. The agricultural reform led to a rapid increase of farm production and the successive industry reform greatly advanced the development of technology. All this was encouraging. However, many problems emerged. The over-stimulated economy caused abnormal rises in prices and national financial difficulties. Thus the government started to limit the development of the economy. After two or three years, the restraint was lifted.

Now the economy is increasing at a remarkable speed. But there lies a crisis behind this prosperity. Corruption is always the big problem that the central government battles with. Though the government has taken various actions to prevent corruption, things still get worse and worse. In fact corruption seems part of the essential system and in factories and business corruption is a disgusting worm. Some persons take advantage of their power to grab as many benefits as possible. They abuse power to such an extent that people have become accustomed to such abuse. At the same time, dozens of speculators appear. They bribe government officials and as a return get many privileges and soon fill their pockets with money.

The open policy is surely very beneficial. Our exports and imports increase every year, which accelerates the building of the Four Modernizations. Advanced technology and administrative experiences of Western countries are continually being introduced into China, which improves our industry standard. But many undesirables also come. The drug addicts and the prostitutes who had vanished after liberation appear again. Adoration of money and the neglect of virtue exist to a serious extent.

Perhaps these things always follow economic increase. But they also have something to do with the government's strategies. I will now discuss another aspect, Chinese education reform, as proof of poor government strategies.

Education is vital to a country. The government is apparently aware of this, but pays insufficient attention to it. I have lived in a city for nearly 20 years. In my district of the city there were three book stores five years ago while there is only one left now, and part of it has also become a clothes store. However, the individual sale of magazines, novels, pictures books, and papers at the street corners increases. Few famous books by authors such as Shakespeare or Einstein can be seen. Many cultural clubs are changed into stores and healthy public entertainment quietly dies away. In school, things are not so good, either. The low salary of teachers drives away many able young people from teaching posts, which makes it hard to improve the teaching quality. Obviously the lack of teaching finance is responsible for this but the government has never solved the problem. On the other side the education reform doesn't have a systematic and practicable theory to follow. Even a schoolmaster doesn't know what school education will be like in two years. What then will a student do to deal with this condition?

Education reform is absolutely necessary, I'm sure of that. But how to carry it out is the problem. The government should carefully consider every aspect and establish a balanced system which makes the process steady. Especially in this modern scientific epoch, the position education should be placed in is a problem that is of central concern to the future of our country.

—**Wu Xu**
International Finance
HENAN PROVINCE

IF YOU ASKED ME before I set foot on Chinese soil to name the three best known symbols of China, I would have said the Chinese national flag, the Great Wall, and the many manifestations of the Chinese dragon. Once here, I discovered a fourth symbol, in Shanghai. Of course, for several good reasons this symbol will never grow to rival the other three; nonetheless, for me it had special significance.

The most memorable landmarks in Shanghai are the elegant new TV tower and the nearby stately promenade which lies between the old European buildings in the Bund and the Huangpu River—that incredibly old gray-and-yellow waterway strewn with marine cranes and every imaginable river craft and sea-going vessel.

It was while crossing the Huangpu on one of the huge, high-suspension bridges that I spied this emblem of modern China. This was in January 1997, and I was on my way to a Chinese wedding. I looked across to the Pudong, Shanghai's vast, new commercial heartland. I saw nothing but construction from horizon to horizon, especially hundreds of industrial cranes. Construction is China's second biggest industry and the crane is its symbol. To me it's the symbol of modern China.

In cities, cranes are everywhere, as are piles of building materials, endless holes in roads, mounds of dirt, industrial ditches, and new telecommunication lines. For millions of rural laborers capable of wielding a shovel or pick, construction signifies hope, so they flood into the cities looking for work. At Beida, on my regular fitness walks around campus, I marveled at the speed and industry of these construction workers. They lived on-site in primitive conditions. Their toil was unremitting. Round the clock they contributed their part to the building process: concrete foundations or walls, scaffolding, window fitting, roofing, painting. I especially admired the craftsmanship in the ornamental bracketing and paintwork around roof lines and upturned eaves. Official figures claim there were 30 million such laborers in 1995, which was 20 percent more than 1994. And the numbers grow and grow. Many commentators claim the numbers are now well over 100 million and rising quickly.

What is disturbing however is that, as well as rural workers, retrenched skilled workers from bankrupt state-owned enterprises and other socially dispossessed people were clearly on the increase. It is a difficult problem to deal with as far too many people are underemployed, but no one wants to be unemployed. In many cities I saw lots of people from this floating population wandering the streets. As a consequence, life in Chinese cities is not quite as safe as it used to be.

Jia Jiangtao now gives his opinion about the "tide of laborers," an opinion which is a little more optimistic than mine.

THE TIDE OF LABORERS IN CHINA

"The tide of laborers" is a new Chinese phrase, created in the late 1980s when large numbers of rural laborers started pouring into China's cities.

China has the largest labor force in the world, but not enough farmland for them to work on. If the rural laborers leave home to find work, they can earn several times the salary they get working in the fields. Such dreams have encouraged many rural laborers to leave their hometowns for the big cities such as Beijing, Shanghai, and Guangzhou. Shenzhen also has been home to about one million outside laborers over the past decade.

Economic reforms in the country have improved efficiency in farming and provided farmers with the means to make their own decisions, even the option to give up agriculture. Meanwhile, China's boom has offered the rural laborers many opportunities.

One benefit of this tide is higher personal incomes for those rural laborers who move into the cities. For the countryside, the outflow of laborers makes it possible for agricultural resources to be redistributed within smaller numbers, to benefit those who have stayed behind. For those in the cities, they can get services and products from rural laborers at relatively cheaper prices. Migrating workers have also filled the demand of those enterprises who might have found themselves in a predicament with the rise in labor costs.

However, the tide of rural workers also has negative effects. Since the laborers are unorganized and migrate at about the same time and usually to the same places, they are a great burden on public transportation. Every year, Spring Festival sees the greatest flow, when public transportation in big cities like Beijing, Guangzhou, and Shanghai finds it difficult to cope. The arrival of rural laborers also creates problems for civil administrations, and crime rates have risen in some areas. Some laborers have suffered from terrible diseases which have spread very quickly among them.

A key to the problem is to develop Chinese agriculture on a broader and deeper level and to develop rural industrial enterprises and urbanization so as to expand employment in the countryside. In addition, the establishment of a unified and ordered national labor market may be a kind of solution. I really hope that the tide will become an ebb tide someday.

—Jia Jiangtao
Geography
JILIN PROVINCE

Perhaps China's greatest challenge is maintaining political stability and continuity. In the mid to late 1990s as East Asia rises even higher as an industrial powerhouse and communist dogma becomes an empty shell, the current conservative leaders continue to trade good economic figures for another week, another month, another year in power. Externally, in addition to the overblown news about the return of Hong Kong and Macao, China's sovereign claims in Taiwan or the various islands in the South China Sea continue to attract world headlines. Internally, the current leaders shore up their position by diverting some funding and turning the rhetoric of growth away from special economic zones along the coast towards the China heartland—the poorer inland provinces.

Insofar as I could tell, in the minds and hearts of most of my students and most of my friends, the belief in the innate unity of the Chinese realm remains intact. It is one of the great continuities of world history and preoccupations of contemporary political life within China and without.

In a prosperous China of two hundred years ago, Emperor Qianlong once informed a British envoy that China was in no need of goods from abroad. After that time, the opium trade, more and more forced foreign concessions, and a reluctance of the Chinese leadership to recognize dangers and adapt to new opportunities caused a gradual one hundred year decline.

Today, the successors to Qianlong sign new business deals with an endless procession of eager Heads of State from every country. Today, Chinese and global commercial interests buttress the political establishment. Now, with the reunification of Hong Kong, China will be the world's fourth biggest trader—after the European Union, U.S.A., and Japan. Ten or more years ago China was a less attractive and necessary world market. It was easier then for Western countries to maintain the high ground condemning China, using principles shaped by Western interpretations of rights and freedoms. Violations and abuses have not disappeared. The difference now for governments and big business is that there are too many zeros at stake.

To the pragmatic Chinese the signs of hope are in factories churning out better quality labor-saving devices, or shirts, or computer software. To many of them a little prosperity is more immediate and practical than progress with individual or community rights.

Nevertheless, underneath economic progress and the veneer of modernization rumbles the pains and uncertainties of social revolution. Which direction will such changes take? Western experiences are useless signposts. We do learn lessons from history, but history doesn't really replicate itself, especially across cultures. I believe that it is scarcely conceivable that social change in China will head down the path of capitalist pluralism—a path we began to take over 400 years ago, at the time of the Reformation.

Why do I say this? Well, some strains of Tibetan Buddhism notwithstanding, China has no history of separation of Church and State. There has been no equivalent to the Western Christian Church. China is not at all like Europe where from the early 1500s the Catholic Church spilt into different Christian segments which lent their weight to what became a bloody fragmentation of Western Europe into more or less interdependent countries. Over those 400 years the split in Christianity lent its weight as well to the development of Western capitalism, individualism, and our notions of privacy. I see no parallel developments in China. I hear the distant thunder of social change in China but hesitate to make any predictions.

For the post-Mao generation and their forebears the lessons of history are more recent and closer to home. Their families have seen far worse experiences: utter poverty, famine, social chaos, and the horrors of totalitarianism. The students have heard stories from the lips of their own relatives who have experienced terror and great suffering—when all semblance of law and order have broken down. What the ordinary Chinese people, the *laobaixing*, worry about is further chaos. What they want above all is stability.

In these circumstances, I wish my Chinese friends good fortune, especially my students and all young people of the post-Mao generation.

*   *   *

As the year 2000 approaches, we in the West depend more and more on a stable and prosperous China. Where do the post-Mao generation believe their country is headed under its policy of "reform and opening?" As might be expected of bright young people at China's premier university, many of my students were very optimistic about their own future and China's future?"

In this next essay, Cao Huachuan gives us his view. I wonder whether you share his optimism as we, the peoples of the world, prepare to enter the new millennium?

CHINA: THE 21ST CENTURY SUPERPOWER

China is the most populous and ancient country in the world. Since liberation in 1949, China has gradually taken on an absolutely new look. But besides glorious moments, there were dark periods of misfortune and calamity. For example, in the 1960s the unprecedented Cultural Revolution pressed catastrophe and sufferings on the Chinese. So in the late 1970s, the elites of our nation eventually conducted serious campaigns against poverty, which marked a historic turning point and inaugurated a new era in China's socialist development.

To intensify the reforming and accelerate the pace of progress further, the Chinese government implemented new measures in 1992 and 1993, such as setting up more special trade zones and shifting to the market economy. Being the largest latent market on earth, the Chinese market is most attractive and lucrative to foreign investors and merchants. Because of her unlimited work force, related abundant resources, and advantageous geographical location, the chances are good for China to develop her own industry and commerce. The increase in Chinese GNP continues and everybody has become much better-off and confident of a promising future.

Establishing closer diplomatic relationships with more countries, pending re-entering the GATT, China has played a more and more important role in world affairs and is regarded as an indispensable force in maintaining peace, stability and prosperity in the Asian and Pacific region. When confronted with bullying U.S.A. or flamboyant U.K., China always depends on her independence and dignity, never giving in against her will or forsaking former principles under unreasonable pressure.

In 1997 and 1999, China will resume the sovereignty of Hong Kong and Macao, so the stigma of being colonized will be gone forever. It also goes without saying that the Taiwan Straits can't separate the mainland and the island which are both occupied by descendants of the same ancestors. In the long run, there is no doubt that China, united as a whole, will become a superpower in 21st century.

Being a young student, I take pride in my motherland and look forward to the realization of such wonderful dream!

—**Cao Huachuan**
Technical Physics
HUNAN PROVINCE

FOR THEIR LAST ESSAY I asked my students to project themselves into China's future, their future, beyond the year 2000. "Imagine," I said, "it is now September, 2000, and the Olympic Games have just commenced in Sydney, Australia. Write a letter to a friend, your parents, me, or anyone about what you are doing. Write about your life, your career, and China."

So the students wrote about their dreams. I have chosen three so you can see what they imagined. Then, because dreams need to come to terms with reality, I will then tell you a little bit about what actually happens to each story-teller upon graduation.

 Chemistry Department
Columbia University
New York State, U.S.A.

August 22, 2000

Dear Mr. Tony,
I am glad to hear from you and to know you're in good health. The good times in the past impressed me much. It was you who opened my eyes to Australia. I still remember the amusing expression on your face when you referred in disgust to those large Australian sugar cane toads.

Now, as a professor in the Chemistry department at Columbia University, I teach undergraduate students organic chemistry. In addition, I spend much time on my research work.

My chemistry students are intelligent, quickly grasping the main idea of each theory, but there is still something left to be desired. I don't expect them to be study machines, so I am trying my best to help them develop their potential to be more creative, imaginative, and considerate. Being with my students, I believe I am young, too, for they always bring so many interesting stories to share with me.

After class I usually go to my laboratory. When I was a teenager, I began to dream about a laboratory of my own. Now it comes true. An assistant helps me type my papers and collect related research materials, so I can do my work whole-heartedly. The peace and quiet in the lab brings to me wings of imagination to roam in the cosmos. I look for the underlying relations between two kinds of phenomena, using experiences to test my hypothesis. I really enjoy my job.

I live in a white house in the suburb 30 miles away from the center of the city. My husband painted it white. In front of the house are lovely lawns and beautiful trees. For relaxation we may mow the lawn or just sit on the lawn talking freely. It is a matter of routine for me to feed my Dana, a 13-month-old dog. She is beautiful, with a golden coat, white chest and stomach. Whenever I walk to her, she'll look at me wagging her tail.

Last month I went to attend an academic meeting in China. The great changes in recent years made me very excited. Cars crowd the highways, telephones are available everywhere, computers are widely used in aviation, medicine, and even in the family. Guess what's happened? Lights on bicycles are compulsory now at night. It is wonderful! It seems as if there were many fireflies flying to and fro.

What surprised me most is the changes in the countryside. Machines now provide most of the power, so it is easier for peasants to produce more food with less labor. As a result, the living standards of the country women have greatly improved, for labor only provides a small part of the power.

I took many photographs during my vacation in China. Some will be sent to you, so you'll have a chance to know what China is like nowadays. I hope you'll enjoy them.

With best wishes,

Liu Jian

DURING 1995 LIU WAS A MONITOR in my Saturday morning class. She came from Sichuan, and was one of the most beautiful and dignified of all the students I taught. She was very bright, too, and ultimately graduated in 1997 as the second best student in her Chemistry year.

As she came to visit me from time to time, I knew she had applied for graduate scholarships in the U.S. Late one lovely spring afternoon in May 1997, as I was riding my bicycle past the old administrative building near Weiming Lake, I saw her approaching me. She was returning to her dorm from the Chemistry laboratory. We stopped to chat. I discovered that the lovely house with the lawns, the husband and the dog may not actually materialize for Liu, but by the year 2000 she is likely to have graduated at doctoral level from one of the world's best universities.

"Yes, I got some scholarship offers," she said.

"So where are you going?" I asked. It was not Columbia after all.

"Yale," she replied.

IN THIS SECOND STORY, Tian Daxiao, a biology student whose hometown of Shijiazhuang is just south of Beijing, writes a letter to a friend. Tian dreams of studying abroad too, after which, he declares with a surge of patriotism, he intends returning to serve China.

 No.1, Hongqi Street
Shijiazhuang
Hebei Province

Sept. 1, 2000

Dear Mo,

I came back at last! Do you want to congratulate me on finishing my postgraduate study and getting the Master's degree after three hard years in America? Two weeks ago, as soon as I got off the plane, I breathed deeply in order to feel our atmosphere, not America's. I went shopping, not only to buy something, but also to talk with people in Chinese.

Before I got ready to come back, I wrote to some research institutes and received several letters of appointment. So, in the last two weeks I visited some of them. I'm very surprised that some middle cities in our province (such as Shijiazhuang) have changed a lot. I can hardly believe it! Do you remember what the city was like in 1996 when we were students at Beida? Shijiazhuang was big, but the roads were dirty and narrow and the traffic was very crowded. Many factories were facing difficulty and workers had nothing to do and couldn't get the basic wages to support their families. But now after the reform and all the citizens' efforts the city has taken on a new look. Roads are widened and huge buildings can be seen. The state enterprises are thriving and the output value of factories is developing at full speed. People's living standards are increasing fast. Father and mother have moved into a new house and Kai and I are planning to buy one. These things we couldn't imagine in the old times.

You want to know what my choice is, don't you? Well, I have decided to go to Hebei Medical Research Institute. There are many highly qualified graduates in the Institute, so this must be a challenging job. I would like to rise to the challenge.

Do you remember the things that happened three years ago? I graduated from the Biology Department of Peking University. You said to me: "You should go abroad for further study and I believe you are able to do so. You are the best of all that I know." Because of your words, I regained confidence and I went overseas to America while Hong Kong was taken back to our motherland.

From then on, I have never lost heart. Whenever I met with trouble, I remembered your words as if you were standing before me. And then I tried my best to overcome problems. I believe your words will go along with me while I am on the road to success. This is one reason that I write to you. I want to give all my thanks to you.

I will go to work tomorrow. My task is to improve medicines used to cure cancer. I hate cancer for it has killed so many people. In America, I read a lot of books about it and did several experiments. Just because of this, I was invited to return home.

What have you been doing these years? I was too busy to write to you in America. I wish you can forgive me. If you can write to me and tell me something about your life, I will be very glad. I am eager for your letter.

Yours,

Tian Daxiao

TIAN WAS ALSO AMONG THE BEST in his year and, like Liu, expected to receive an offer of a scholarship. For one reason or another, his expectations were not realized. So, when I met him during my last semester I expected him to be rather disconsolate. But he was not. He told me he had plans to continue into graduate school in 1998, probably in Beijing. In the meantime he would obtain work in Shijiazhuang through his parents' associates.

After saying this, Tian smiled at me and asked me whether I could recall teaching my students "Life's Little

Instructions?" (In each English lesson the students would have a five minute small group discussion on the meanings of three or four of "Life's Little Instructions," which I got from a book with the same name.) So I said "Of course, I do," and asked him what he was really trying to say.

He told me that one instruction I explained in class encouraged him to never give up on his dreams. Then he said he never would give up. I remembered the Little Instruction:

Never give up on what you really want to do. The person with big dreams is more powerful than one with all the facts.

In the third and final story you are about to read, Shao Yue imagines she becomes a reporter for the *China Daily* and travels to Australia just before the Olympics. Shao Yue was an International Finance Department student. You have already read her poignant story, "My Country Childhood," in Chapter 2. When I left China in 1997, Shao Yue had just graduated and was on an Australian banking company's shortlist of possible new recruits. I hope they chose her. She would be an excellent investment.

Her story also contains glowing visions of how Beida will grow and prosper. This latter wish matches objectives set by the Senior University Administration and the State Education Commission. As I left China the signs that this was beginning to happen were obvious. Peking University was putting on its most beautiful face for 1998, its centenary year.

China Daily
Beijing, China

September 3, 2000

Dear Xinwei,

Last night, I had a dream. We went back to Peking University in the dream. I wore that gingham frock like before. We walked around Weiming Lake. All of a sudden, I woke up. It was midnight. I'm in Beijing, while you are in Washington, U.S.A.

How time flies! We haven't seen each other for three years! As you know, I dreamed of becoming a reporter when I was a student at Peking University. I hoped that one day I could travel to many places and record the great changes in China. Now my dream has come true. I take pride in my career. Of course, sometimes I am tired. As a reporter, you have to face a lot of challenges and change with this changing world, I often stay up late. But tonight I'm not working. I am listening to the old Carpenter's song, "Yesterday Once More," while drinking coffee. The vapor from the coffee blurs my eyes. I miss you. Can you feel my loneliness tonight?

Do you still remember the little girl in Anhui Province to whom we offered tuition every term? Recently I went to Anhui and met her. She is now a pretty girl and always gets top marks in her middle school. To my great joy, she is very fond of literature. She does have an aptitude for it. She dreams of studying in the Chinese Department as we used to. Most students in that Hope School study well. Project Hope has been carried out for ten years. With the development of economy and education, all children will study happily.

Last year, I went to Sydney, Australia, where

the Olympic Games is being held. We did dream it would be held in Beijing. Finally we lost the opportunity. But Sydney is really a very beautiful city. Walking on the sandy beach, I thought of you. You must know by now that the Olympic Games of 2004 will be held in China. Beijing is getting more and more beautiful and the people are all ready for the guests from all over the world.

To my surprise, I met with our English teacher, Mr. Tony. Among many people on the beach, we recognized each other nearly at the same time. He had not changed a lot, but time has changed me much. My eyes became misty. I hadn't help thinking of those old golden days. Yet smiles lit up Mr. Tony's face. He asked me again and again, "How is Peking University? How is China?" His words reminded me of your letter.

You always ask me over and over, "How is our Peking University? How is our China?" Dear, great changes have taken place both at Peking University and in China. A new report shows that Peking University has become the best university in Asia, while she was in fifth place in 1995. A new International Students College was officially opened in June as part of the celebrations for the 100th anniversary of our university. If only you were here now, so we could stroll around campus as we did five years ago! The campus has taken on a new look. Weiming Lake and the Boya Pagoda are still the most attractive features. As a fine art student you would be fascinated by the unique design of the magnificent new library in the central square. It's said to be the largest university library in Asia. I can't believe that, can you?

As for China, I feel I can't describe her well in a letter. Autumn, the most beautiful season in Beijing, has come. Would you like to come back? In addition, we can go back to Changsha, to our hometown. Is that okay?

Ah, it's midnight. Looking out of the window, I saw the stars twinkling in the sky. But it is noon in Washington. What are you doing now? You are far away from me! Do you know a new day is coming in Beijing?

Looking forward to your letter...

Yours ever,

Shao Yue

Peking University, 20 July 1997

OVER FOUR YEARS AGO, on a cold winter's day in January 1993, I stood for the first time on the beautiful old stone bridge just inside Peking University's West Gate. Today, on a warm summer's evening in late July 1997, I walk slowly across campus to stand once more on that old bridge for the last time.

I look across to the ancient grassed entrance area within the university. Adjacent to the square with its ornately carved Qing dynasty twin stone pillars, I see many workmen continuing their external renovations on some of Beida's oldest buildings—the Oriental Languages building and my building, the English Department. Tomorrow I am leaving China. Meanwhile life goes on, as it must. The university is preparing for its one hundredth birthday. Yes, not only am I leaving a different university, I am leaving a different China.

I thought that despite all the calamities and cruelties since 1949, China has maintained its unity, redistributed its land and wealth, and cleaned out those centuries-old layers of parasitic special interests that stunt growth. Although, sadly, it seems now that parasitic layers are on the march again. I thought too that with my Western eyes I do not see China as a free country, but today its people can and do strike out on their own as entrepreneurs and, within greater constraints than I am used to, as citizens.

Since the initial golden days of Maoism and Marxism, and the subsequent disorder and oppression, old ideological hopes have grown pale and old sanctions have weakened. China is no longer monolithic. Can it ever be again? Fear is shrinking amidst its people. That makes a huge difference to a nation's well-being. Chinese people now live far better than they have before. It gave me deep joy to think that, given favorable political winds and the avoidance of major natural disasters, China now has the chance to grow and prosper.

I suddenly remember what my students said to me in my first semester: Mr. Tony faces to the south. For some time I had been longing for home, for my family, for Annette. It was comforting beyond expression to know that she and they were eagerly awaiting my return to Canberra, to Australia. I recall a Chinese proverb the students once told me: "Being reunited after some time apart surpasses being married for the first time."

I realize my students, my windows into China, helped me not only to see their country and its people, but also to see deeply into myself. I am different too. I feel stronger. One day I will come back.

Also from China Books—

For anyone who would like to live, work or study in China, this unique and badly needed book should be considered indispensable . . . . This book may well become to the foreign residents in China what THE JOY OF COOKING has been to newlyweds.

—Mark Salzman,
author of IRON AND SILK

Full of helpful advice and practical information for those studying or teaching in China. . . . The authors are amusingly frank on the hardships and heartaches of surviving, working (and dating) in China.

—Jonathan Spence

LIVING IN CHINA:
A GUIDE TO TEACHING AND STUDYING IN CHINA, INCLUDING TAIWAN & HONG KONG

Rebecca Weiner, Margaret Murphy, and Albert Li

The bestselling guide to finding a school in China is back, with expanded listings and new, updated advice for students and teachers. Schools in China vary widely with regard to salaries, class size, number of foreigners, living conditions, and other variables that can make the difference between a great experience and one that leaves you longing for home.

LIVING IN CHINA shows how to search for the right school, contact names, telephone numbers, web sites, and e-mail addresses, with frank comments by people who have lived there. Great reference for those planning extended business trips or travel as well. Appendices include schools in China, US sending institutions, key foreign contacts, embassies, bibliography, and much more.

 TRAVEL
China Books, 1997
6" x 8"
0-8351-2582-3

300pp
$19.95

VISIT US ON
THE WORLD WIDE WEB!

Don't wait for our catalog to come in the mail, point your web browser to our new URL:
http://www.chinabooks.com

Visit our web site for up-to-the-minute listings of new books, titles not available in our catalogs, and lots of other China-related information.

- Read excepts and sample chapters from new books.
- Browse our expanded catalog.
- Learn more about China Books & Periodicals
- Get up-to-date information about China-related news and events.
- Link-up to other web sites.
- Check out our bulletin board.
- Participate in contests and win prizes.
- Download free clip art images.
- Get additional information on our products.
- Take advantage of our monthly specials.
- Find new information about China—recipes, quotes, projects and more.

Concerned about secure ordering? Call or E-mail us about setting up an on-line account.

Have a China-related book or product you would like to promote? Set up a web page or advertise on the China Books web site. Call us for more information.